THE CONCISE DICTIONARY
OF INTERIOR DECORATING

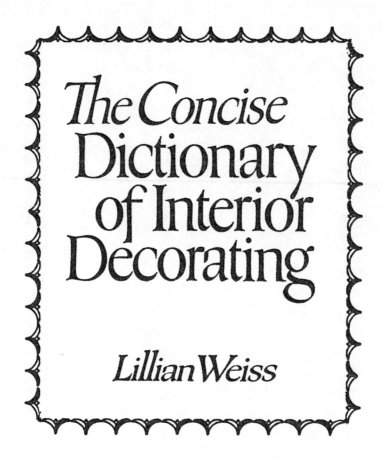

The Concise Dictionary of Interior Decorating

Lillian Weiss

DOUBLEDAY & COMPANY, INC., GARDEN CITY, N.Y.

ISBN: *0-385-05163-8*
Library of Congress Catalog Card Number 72–89358
Copyright © 1973 by Margaret R. Weiss
Copyright © 1971 by Nelson Doubleday, Inc.

AUTHOR'S NOTE

No matter in what language it is printed or to which specialized subject it applies, a dictionary must define—briefly and precisely—the words within its specific framework. In this instance, the subject encompasses design and decoration, and the vocabulary is the richly descriptive one that details the life story of our decorative environment.

From initial word selection to final compilation of definitions, we have had one aim in view: the creation of a handy guide—compact enough for quick, easy reference, yet comprehensive enough to cover the major facets of its manifold subject.

Accordingly, we weighed and winnowed the items to be included for definition. Focusing on basic terms and essential concepts, we bypassed words that have no specific application to decoration—such terms as *entablature, architrave, façade,* for example, which relate principally to architecture and can be found in any standard college-type dictionary. Similarly, words that are part of our daily language (*artificial flowers, bor-*

der, etc.) were also omitted because in decorating terminology they hold no additional meaning beyond their usual connotation. Nor have we included certain other words like *cresset, astrolabe, posset pot,* as they are mainly pertinent to the ardent antiquarian or historian rather than the general information seeker.

Like the vade-mecum foreign-language phrasebook that reassures the traveler abroad, this dictionary is designed to meet the practical tests of everyday use. The words defined should enable today's homemaker to make meaningful dialogue with the world of the designer and interior decorator, with the books and magazines that offer home-decorating ideas and inspiration, and with the resources where items for the home are displayed and sold.

For those who consider a dictionary merely an appetite whetter, the suggested bibliography at the back of the book will be a guide to further exploration into the fascinating, sometimes controversial, always rewarding landscape of interior design and decoration.

Lillian Weiss
New York

5

THE CONCISE DICTIONARY
OF INTERIOR DECORATING

A B C

A

Abstract Art Contemporary art form based on the juxtaposition of colors, shapes, mass and line; geometric arrangements of essential forms; non-representational in content, non-realistic in execution.

Acanthus A leaf motif used decoratively since ancient times. It was characteristic ornamentation of Corinthian columns. The leaf is sketched or carved in a stylized manner, often in multiple overlapping effects; its popularity increased during the eighteenth-century revival of classicism.

Accents A contrasting color or a selection of accessories used within a decorative scheme to dramatize certain details; e.g., a neutral scheme accented by a sharp color to intensify the effect of the subtle tones; an Early American setting highlighted by pewter accessories to emphasize the period, etc.

Acetate All-purpose fiber derived from a chemical (salt of acetic acid); mixed with other fibers it is in general use for flat and pile fabrics; acetate taffeta, for example, has a smooth lustrous feel, sheds wrinkles, takes well to dyes.

ACANTHUS

Acrylic Plastic There are three commonly used versions: as fiber for fabrics of all types and constructions, as sheet plastic (frequently transparent) for furniture and accessories, and as an ingredient of household paint. In all

11

cases, acrylics (under such registered trade names as Acrilan, Creslan, Orlan, Plexiglas, Lucite, etc.) have many fine features: in woven fabrics, stain and moth-resistance, fast drying; stability; sheet acrylics are tough, can be used structurally (room dividers, etc.) and for furniture; in paint, acrylic content gives hardness and permanence.

Adam, Robert (England, 1728–92)
Together with his brothers James and William, a talented trio of English architects who designed complete decorative schemes as well as the furnishings to go into them; Robert was appointed chief architect to King George III in 1762; Adam styles are characterized by the graceful classical motifs that

ADAM DESIGNS

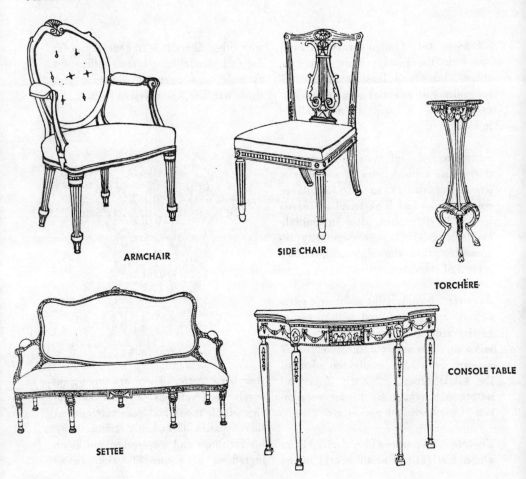

ARMCHAIR

SIDE CHAIR

TORCHÈRE

SETTEE

CONSOLE TABLE

were then being unearthed in Rome and Pompeii; applied swags and garlands in Wedgwood-like carvings; satinwood and light mahogany rather than the heavy dark woods like oak and walnut.

Adaptation   A copy of an earlier design but not necessarily with all of the authentic details which go into making a reproduction piece; e.g., a Chippendale-style sofa made into a dual-purpose sofa bed; a narrow-width original fabric rescaled for printing on a 54-inch width ground cloth.

Adirondack Furniture   Porch or garden furniture including slant-backed arm chairs made of natural-finished redwood slats; strong and weather resistant.

ADIRONDACK CHAIR

Age of Oak, Walnut, Mahogany, Satinwood   The woods used during various periods of English furniture design. The Age of Oak flourished from 1500–1600; the Age of Walnut, from 1660–1720; the Age of Mahogany, 1720–65; the Age of Satinwood, 1765–1800.

Alabaster   Translucent mineral rang-

ing in color from off-white to rust; used mainly for lamp bases, small sculptures, bookends, paperweights and other accessories; it chips easily even though it is dense and heavy.

Alpujarra Rug   A handmade area rug from southern Spain; intricately knotted, heavy wool fringe borders all sides; reversible and often used as a wall hanging; patterns are of peasant origin and range from two-tone to full-color effects.

Amberina Glass   A two-colored American glass made from 1883 to the turn of the century; pale amber shading up to deep ruby red; made by several factories including the famous New England Glass Company; the glass has great luster and is used generally for accessories and serving pieces.

American Indian Rugs   Navajo rugs hand-woven on Southwest reservations; colorful primitive motifs in clear primary colors; geometric stripes and borders; flat weaves.

Amorini   These are happy little cupids and cherubs used as applied decoration; they may be fully sculptured or carved in bas-relief; a late seventeenth-century fashion.

Analogous Colors   Any series of colors, usually at least three, that are adjacent on the color wheel, i.e., yellow, yellow-green, green.

Anchor Mark   This symbol is found at the base of pottery and porcelain objects and identifies wares made by the

Chelsea, Derby, or Bow factories; it is also the mark that confirms a solid silver piece even if no other symbol is engraved.

ANCHOR MARKS

Andirons Also called firedogs, they are metal (usually iron) bars made to hold logs within the fireplace.

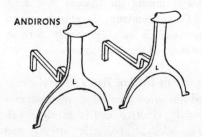

ANDIRONS

Anthemion, or Honeysuckle, Motif Ancient Greek and Roman design applied to many objects from pottery to buildings; Hepplewhite simplified the basic form for use as a chair back.

ANTHEMION

Antimacassars Crocheted or tatted doilies used on chair backs and arms to protect fabrics from the marks left by the oily, macassar hair-dressing lotion liked by Victorian dandies.

Antique Any object that is one hundred or more years old may, according to a U. S. Government ruling, be called an antique.

Antique Satin Random slubs on a smooth weave; may be of silk, rayon, cotton, acetate, etc.; has a shiny surface and tailors well for draperies, bedspreads, and upholstery.

Apostle Spoons A complete set of thirteen Antique English spoons, bearing as handles the sculptured representation of Christ and the twelve disciples; figures are full length; dating from the fifteenth century, they were originally designed as christening spoons.

Apothecary Jar Glass, porcelain, or earthenware container to hold herbs and drugs; variously decorated and labeled in colors or in metallic gold and black; originally, used exclusively by pharmacists from the seventeenth through the nineteenth centuries; present-day copies are widely seen as decorative accessories.

Appliqué An applied trim which may be cut out of one fabric and sewed to another for contrast of color, texture, pattern; in furniture, it is brass, ormolu, or carved wood decoration that is glued or screwed to the surface.

Apron That section of table which goes horizontally just below the top; with or without a drawer; on a chair, it is the band just below the seat.

APRON

Arabesque A design motif from the Near East, popular in Europe since the Renaissance; especially popular during the eighteenth century; formed of interlacing vines, leaves, garlands, and flowers traced in either monotone or full-color effects.

Architectural Lighting Non-portable lighting indicated on the blueprint or actual building plan; incorporated as an integral element of the structure.

Area, or Accent, Rug As its name suggests, a small rug whose shape, colors, or boldness of pattern bring a note of interest to a setting; perhaps under a glass-topped coffee table, or to enliven a dark corner, etc.

Armoire The French word for wardrobe, but the kind used for storing clothing before the days of built-in closets; originally, used to store armor; a seventeenth-century innovation currently popular in Provincial decorative schemes.

Armpad Small upholstered pad matching the chair upholstery; used as an armrest on French period chairs and frequently seen on Victorian sofas and chairs.

Arraiolo Rug A Portuguese hand-embroidered accent rug; coarse cross-stitch embroidery which may be colorfully contemporary or delicately pastel and traditional; backed with linen; these artistically colored little rugs can often be the inspiration for an entire room's color scheme.

Arras A woven wall tapestry first made in Arras, a city in northern France, in the fourteenth and fifteenth centuries; the word was adopted into the English language and has become a generic term for tapestry.

Art Nouveau (1890–1910) Flowing lines, gentle curves, and Japanese influences mark this forerunner of Art Moderne styles of the 1920s; perfect examples of the form may be seen in Tiffany's Favrile glass objects; the words are French and mean new art.

Ash Moderately hard wood with an oaklike grain; light gray to warm brown color; moisture resistant; used for medium-priced case furniture, kitchen cabinets, concealed parts like drawer backs and sides.

ARMOIRE

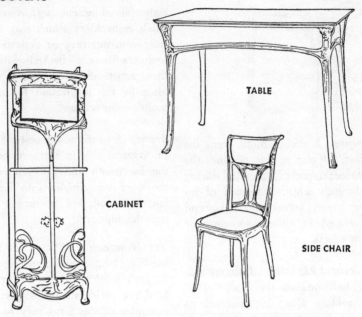

TABLE

CABINET

SIDE CHAIR

Atrium An open inner court, sometimes with center pool, around which the living quarters of the ancient Roman and Greek houses were constructed; a terrazzo-paved walk; hedge or flower border often surrounded the atrium.

Aubusson Rug French in concept and manufacture ever since the factory's founding in the eighteenth century; the Aubusson weave (also used for tapestry) resembles needlepoint; usually has a pale ivory or cream ground with floral design and arabesques in pastel tints of rose, blue, green, lavender, beige.

Audubon Prints Reproductions of the fine drawings and paintings of native American birds by the famed naturalist John J. Audubon. The limited editions of the original engravings, made in London from 1828 to 1837, are found mainly in museum collections.

Austrian Shade A curtain that is shirred in scalloped panels; pulled up like a window shade, it needs no rollers. Since Austrian shades are very decorative, they serve as combined curtains and shades and need no overdrapery to give a finished look to the window. *Roman shades* operate on the same principle except that they are pleated in tailored flat folds; both versions use a system of cords to raise and lower.

Authentic The genuine item whether it is furniture, a decorative object, or an artifact; neither a reproduction nor a copy; stamps, labels, and other marks of origin are valuable proofs of an article's authenticity and should never be removed or defaced.

Avodire   A cream-gold toned wood with ripple markings that run across a medium-fine grain; used for wall paneling, veneers for high-quality case furniture, and as ornamental trim.

Awning Stripe   A broad pattern—at least three inches wide—of alternating color and white stripes; derived from the traditional canvas awning; used for slipcovers and draperies.

Axminster   A rug weave, not a pattern or a quality; when more than five colors are required to delineate a pattern, an Axminster loom is necessary; designs can be complex and elaborate with period styles dominant; an Axminster weave cannot be rolled crosswise but only along its length.

B

Baccarat Fine crystal stemware and decorative accessories made currently in France; sometimes combined with ormolu trim.

Bachelor's Chest A small, four-drawer chest with a pull-out slide just under the top (useful as a writing surface or to hold accessories while dressing); popular storage piece for men during the eighteenth century; often seen today used in pairs as lamp tables, or as generally practical pieces for foyer or entryway. (*See* Federal American Period.)

Baker's Rack Tall, wide *étagère* made of wrought iron, often brass trimmed, and customarily used by French bakers to display their wares; greatly prized by interior designers who find them functional and attractive.

Balance Formal or equal balance places objects of equal size and weight at both sides of a center point (pairs of tables, pairs of lamps, etc.); informal balance uses unmatched objects of equivalent proportions to achieve the harmonious arrangement of varied elements.

Ball Fringe An edge trimming of little pompoms hanging at spaced intervals from a band of woven braid; used on draperies, valances, café curtains, tablecloths, pillows.

Balloon-back Chair A popular Early Victorian chair style; it has an open, horizontal oval frame above a tufted or plain seat; usually armless.

BALLOON-BACK CHAIR

19

Baluster An intricately turned column for chair legs, chair backs, banister posts; a seventeenth-century design.

BALUSTER

Bamboo A tropical tree with hollow, woody stems and branches; used for furniture during the eighteenth-century *chinoiserie* trend, and especially liked in Regency England. The ringed, jointed, streaky pattern of real bamboo was simulated in a variety of materials, often brilliantly lacquered; even ceramics have had a turn at pretend bamboo; the interest continues in present times—wallpaper, vinyl place mats, fabrics printed with bamboo trellis designs, bamboo handles on stainless steel flatware, etc. seem to emphasize this as an enduring style. "Late antique" bamboo hat racks, washstands, and garden furniture of the Victorian era are a collector's quarry.

Banding or Cross-banding A border or edge of contrasting wood; e.g., satinwood with mahogany; cross-banding is set *against* the grain while straight banding is set *along* the grain.

Banjo Clock Pendulum wall clock shaped after the musical instrument; it was designed and made by Simon Willard about 1800.

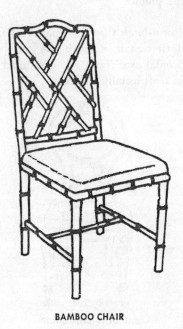

BAMBOO CHAIR

BANJO CLOCK

Banquette Upholstered bench unit with or without back; used against a wall; a favorite type of seating in French restaurants.

20

Barcelona Chair An armless, tufted leather chair set on a sloping X-shaped metal frame; introduced by Mies van der Rohe in 1929, it is considered one of the great classic pieces of contemporary design. (*See* Bauhaus.)

Barometer A device for measuring atmospheric pressure and to forecast weather changes; its banjo shape and old-style lettering are decorative qualities that continue to make the barom-eter an admired wall accessory as well as a functioning instrument.

Baroque Prevalent in all European countries from the mid-sixteenth to the eighteenth century, this vivacious, highly ornate style was based on sweeping curves and volutes, overscaled proportions; the Venetian mirror, huge tufted headboard, and some painted finishes came into favor; although the Baroque was simultaneous with Jacobean and Puritan styles in England, it did not take hold there until after the period of austerity had faded out.

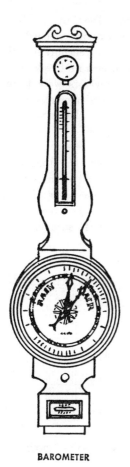

BAROMETER

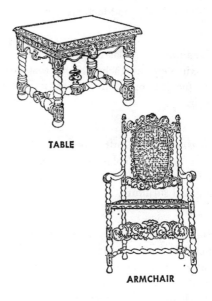

TABLE

ARMCHAIR

Barrel Chair Fully upholstered, high-backed chair that looks like a barrel cut in half; staves are sometimes suggested by vertically channeled tufts in the upholstery.

21

Bas-relief Two-dimensional, sculptured carvings or modeling attached to a background from which they are just slightly raised.

Basalt Ware A smooth-textured, matte-black stoneware made by several potteries, but it is generally associated with the Wedgwood factory.

Baseboard A flat wood molding (approximately six inches high) that covers the joining of the inside wall and floor.

Basswood A soft wood of streaky white to brown color; it does not easily warp; mostly used for inexpensive unfinished furniture.

Batik A dye process that originated in the East Indies, which gives a random-color effect; produced on cotton and used for a variety of fashion items in the home, i.e., draperies, pillows, etc.

Batiste Thin cotton fabric resembling voile but finer and silkier to the touch; also made of synthetic fibers; it is used for softly tailored window curtains.

Bauhaus The German school of architecture and design, opened in 1919 and responsible for encouraging the modern design concepts we live by today; many leading innovators were trained there; it was the fundamental source of clean-lined, functional home furnishings.

Bay Window One that projects from the outside wall of a building and is supported from below; inside, the bay forms a three-sided recess; a *bow* window is similarly structured in a curve.

BAY WINDOW

22

AUHAUS DESIGNS

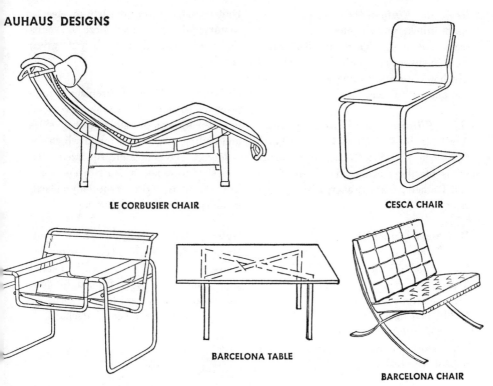

LE CORBUSIER CHAIR

CESCA CHAIR

BARCELONA TABLE

BARCELONA CHAIR

BREUER CHAIR

Bead Curtain Strings of large wood, plastic, or ceramic beads are hung from ceiling, door lintel, or window frame to serve as room dividers in place of solid doors, and as a decorative window curtain; originated in the Far East in the mid-1800s and presently revived.

Beading A type of applied molding that looks like a string of flattened beads; used as trimming on eighteenth- and nineteenth-century furniture.

BEADING

Beaker Easy to grasp because of its tapering cylindrical shape, a drinking cup made without handles; pewter or silver; plain or engraved.

BEAKER

Beamed Ceiling To give the effect of Tudor-period and countrified architecture, wooden ceiling beams are exposed and not plastered over; usually stained in a dark oak tone to contrast with white or pastel-painted ceiling.

23

Beauvais Embroidery A close, tiny chain stitch, machine-made, so fine in scale that it is difficult to distinguish from handwork; multicolor floral motifs, bowknots and monograms on luxury bed and bath linens.

Bed Pillows (size and filling) Available in 17-inch×24-inch, 19-inch ×25-inch, 21-inch×27-inch sizes; many kinds of fillers are used—down, down and feathers, foam rubber, kapok, polyester fiber fills.

Bed Sizes (in widths)
Cot: 30 inches
Single: 33–36 inches
Twin: 39 inches
Three quarters: 48 inches
Double: 54 inches
Queen size: 60–66 inches
King size: 78 inches (equivalent to a pair of twin beds)

Bed Table Different from a bedside table in that it is an adjustable, tray-on-pedestal device that slides over a bed or across a chair; it was first produced in eighteenth-century England as a convenience for invalids. Seen today in hospitals.

Beech A dense, strong furniture wood that bends without snapping, which makes it ideal for all bentwood furniture, structural parts and frames; light brown with reddish tinge.

Belleek China A very thin-bodied translucent, highly glazed porcelain that originated and is still being made in Belleek, Ireland; it was also made in the United States during the late nineteenth century; the pearl-like glaze is sometimes overpainted with bright green shamrocks.

Bellows A piece of fireplace equipment consisting of two shaped wood panels with compressible leather sides and ending in a tube through which air is forced. The panels are squeezed open and shut to create a draft to enliven a fire. Antique styles, especially blacksmith's, are collectors' items.

Belter, John (1795–1865) Mid-Victorian New York City cabinetmaker whose style was florid; heavily carved chairs and sofas were framed in dark rosewood; covers were tufted fabrics or the more uncompromising horsehair.

BELTER CHAIR

Bennington Pottery Earthenware with a characteristic mottled-brown drip glaze; made from about 1825–1900 in Bennington, Vermont; collected by fanciers of antique American pottery.

Bent Glass Flat glass that has been shaped while hot into cylinders and curved objects of various sorts; many contemporary decorative accessories are made this way, then decorated with metallic gold or other color screen-printed motifs.

Bentwood Developed and patented by the Michael Thonet factory (first in Germany, later established in Austria); wood is bent and curved under steam so that furniture may be constructed without joints; actively produced since the mid-nineteenth century and continuing into the present; in fact, contemporary industrial designers are reviving and improving the technique for some of the most modern furniture, eliminating many of the unnecessarily fussy curves that characterize the traditional bentwood styles.

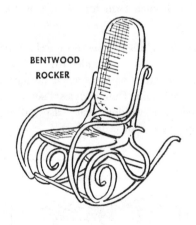

BENTWOOD ROCKER

Bergère An armchair of eighteenth-century French design; upholstered within a surrounding wood frame; fully closed arm. (*See* Louis XV.)

Bessarabian, or Ukrainian, Rug Bessarabia was a former Rumanian province that received the dual influences of Turkish and its own peasant craftsmen; typical designs are sprawling floral motifs woven in a tapestrylike stitch.

Betty Lamp Primitive American hanging oil lamp; oval-shaped with a wick inserted in the narrow end; a long hook was generally part of the lamp itself; also called a phoebe lamp.

Bevel The inner edge of a mirror, glass, or mat board cut on a slant to bring it to the same level as the print or painting to be framed.

Bibelot A decorative accessory that may be somewhat less important than an *objet d'art*; *bibelot* is French for curio, trinket.

Bidet A bathroom convenience used for personal hygiene; Europeans have always considered the bidet essential equipment, and now Americans are beginning to appreciate its usefulness as an aid to cleanliness.

Biedermeier (*Germany and Central Europe, 1810–50*) Simplified, but obvious adaptation of French Empire style; combination of light-finished woods with painted black trim, or fruitwoods with ebony; the emerging, affluent, middle-class society resulting from the Industrial Revolution could afford a "decorator" approach to home fashions, and they more or less adopted this comfortable style as their own.

BIEDERMEIER DESIGNS

CYLINDER DESK

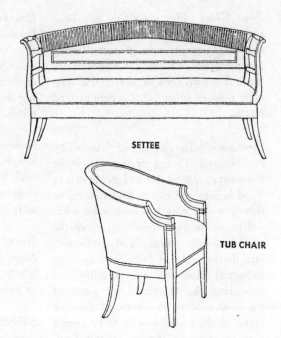

SETTEE

TUB CHAIR

Birch Even-textured, hard wood with lustrous golden-brown tone and a pinkish cast; bleached pale for contemporary, or red-brown for traditional furniture styles; used for both exposed surfaces and concealed parts of furniture.

Bisque Unglazed and undecorated porcelain that has been given only a first firing; soft and velvetlike to the touch, bisque china is an ideal material for figurines and other small sculpture.

Bitters Bottle A slender glass bottle with a long narrow neck and a special kind of stopper that lets flow only one drop at a time; a bar accessory.

Blanc de Chine A very fine white glazed porcelain made in China during the Ming Dynasty; its characteristic whiteness is very slightly tinged with pink rather than with a cooler bluish color. French term for Chinese white.

Blanket Chest Low storage chest with a flat-topped or a rounded lift-up lid; often decorated with stenciled designs in Pennsylvania Dutch styles; sometimes used as a window seat; also called a hope, dower, or cedar chest.

BLANKET CHEST

26

Block Front A chest or desk whose center section is recessed while the two side panels protrude; American eighteenth-century design and construction.

BLOCK FRONT

Blue Glass Liners These were introduced in the 1770s when many pierced-silver table accessories became fashionable; the blue glass offered pleasing contrast; especially typical, the open salt dish still in current manufacture.

Bobèche A small glass saucerlike dish with a center hole set on top of a candlestick to catch dripping wax and protect the base of the stick; sometimes trimmed with crystal pendants or prisms around the edge.

Bohemian Glass First made in the sixteenth century and continuing into the present; characterized by its use of red, green, deep blue, or amber overlay on clear glass; decanters, vases, wine glasses, cordial sets, and other decorative accessories imported or made in the United States; also called cased glass.

Boiserie French for woodwork; a wood paneling—carved or plain, simply stained or wax finished—that covers an entire wall. Typically French eighteenth-century decorative treatment to serve as a subdued but interesting background to colorful furnishings.

Bokara Rug Motifs are frequently octagonal shape or stylized rose; background is traditionally red, but modern rugs are being woven with ivory ground as well; multicolored: turquoise, green, gold, brown; Bokaras are compatible to contemporary interiors and many designers use them as accent notes in neutral-color settings; made in Turkestan, Central Asia.

Bolection A decorative molding that projects outward from wall or paneling; usually ogee shaped (in form of a double S in profile). Used especially to frame fireplace openings.

Bolster Usually, a long cylindrical pillow used at arms and backs of sofas and day beds; also, a slipcover for a bed pillow made to match the bedspread.

Bombé A French word that describes furniture with rounded, swelling front contours; mainly seen on chests and commodes, sometimes on occasional tables.

Bonbonnière Covered candy dish made of porcelain or enameled metal; an authentic French eighteenth-century piece is a collector's item more often displayed in a curio cabinet than put to use.

Bone China Fine china or porcelain

to which bone ash has been added for extra strength and translucence.

Bonnetière Slender, tall cabinet, shelved and grille-doored, designed during the eighteenth century; its original purpose was to house a plumed picture hat on each shelf; today it is used as a curio or china cabinet.

BONNET TOP

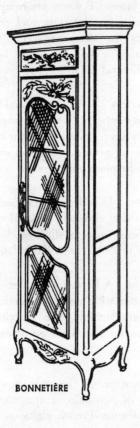

BONNETIÈRE

Bonnet Top A broken pediment with center finial; used to top a chest of drawers, secretary, or highboy; especially American design of late eighteenth-century Federal period.

Borax A term that describes flashy, ornate furniture, poorly constructed and tasteless in design; advertised and promoted by low-end stores, it is no bargain in any circumstances. (*See* also Kitsch.)

Border Print Fabric or wallpaper that is composed of two pattern elements: a narrow section (about one third of the width) has a dense arrangement of motifs; the larger section is made up of repeats of smaller, scattered motifs; the border parallels the length of the fabric or paper.

Boston Rocker An American rocking chair derived from the eighteenth-century English Windsor chair prototype, characterized by a spindle back topped by a wide crest rail which was usually painted or stenciled.

Botanical Print Realistic renderings of floral specimens used as motifs on

28

BOSTON ROCKER

Boulle, or Buhl, André (France, 1642–1732) French cabinetmaker who first introduced many of the style characteristics we recognize as period French; lavish use of inlay patterns made of contrasting woods, metal, tortoise shell; his influence on French and English cabinetmaker colleagues was great.

Bourbon Restoration Period (France, 1815–48) The return of France's hereditary ruling family after Napoleon's fall brought little that was uniquely French to the world of home fashions; most designs paralleled trends set in other centers like London, Vienna, New York.

chintz or other decorative fabrics; small "spriggy" single blooms or bouquets.

Bouclé Woven for upholstery use, bouclé is a looped fabric with depth and roughness of texture; made of all fibers and combinations. French for curled.

Bouillotte Lamp Desk or table lamp in form of single or multiple candleholder; usually metal with a painted metal shade.

Box Edge The right-angle edges of box cushions constructed with corner seams, usually accented with welting or carding.

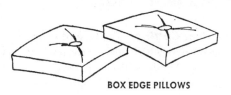

BOX EDGE PILLOWS

Boxwood Light yellowish-colored wood with a distinctive scent used in inlay on furniture; many musical instruments use boxwood in some sections. In its natural state it grows densely and is used for clipped borders and topiary trees in formal gardens.

Bracket Foot Furniture foot whose straight edge lines up with outside, and curved contour faces the inside; notable

BOUILLOTTE LAMP

29

feature of Early American chest and dresser in its simplest form; on eighteenth-century English furniture, the bracket foot is much more elaborately carved.

Brasses All the applied brass door and drawer pulls, knobs, etc. that form part of the decorative trim on a piece of furniture.

Breakfront Large-scale bookcase or china cabinet whose center section protrudes beyond its side sections; usually glass-doored above a cupboard or drawered base; upper shelves display books or accessories; sometimes metal grilles are used in place of glass. (*See* Chippendale.)

Bric-a-brac All the small accessories and objects collected for their sentimental value, curiosity, or rarity; the word is French and very expressive.

Brilliant Cutting The type of cutting done on glass with a power-driven wheel; for deep, highly polished patterns popular during the peak of fashion for cut glass.

Bristol Glass Clear bright shades of turquoise, apple green, or violet; smooth, silky texture; opaque and tough; for decorative ware like candlesticks, vases, boxes, bonbonnières.

Britannia Metal A white alloy developed around 1800; lighter in weight and thinner, it gradually replaced pewter for everyday hollow ware; after 1840 it became the base for electroplated silver.

Broadloom Carpet As the name implies, carpet woven or tufted on a broad loom; widths of 9 feet, 12 feet, 15 feet, and 18 feet are available to fit into average-size rooms without having to be seamed; for wall-to-wall installations and room-size, bound rugs.

Brocade A heavyweight jacquard weave with allover patterns of small florals or geometric motifs; background is satin weave with the designs slightly raised and like embroidery; two-tone, multicolor, and solid color effects; made of various fibers and combinations.

Bronze-doré Metal washed with gilt; used for lighting fixtures, table lamps, desk accessories; and in the eighteenth century, decorative mounts on French furniture; also, ormolu. French for gilded bronze.

Bubble Glass What began as an accident of manufacture—small irregular bubbles scattered throughout an object —has become a technique used purposely for decorative effect.

Buckram A coarse, heavily sized fabric; used as a lining and stiffening inside curtain and drapery headings (the side curtain and drapery headings (the solves in water).

Buffet French for sideboard, a flat-topped cabinet for storage and serving; platters and tureens are placed on it for easy self-service—this was probably the inspiration for "buffet supper" entertaining.

Bull's-eye Mirror Small, round wall mirror with ornamental frame; sometimes has candleholders attached at sides; usually gilded; very prevalent in early eighteenth-century American interiors. (*See* Federal American Period.)

Bun Foot An early seventeenth-century innovation, the bun foot—a flattened ball shape—preceded the claw-and-ball as a decorative terminal to a chair leg.

Bunching Tables Small occasional tables designed to be used singly or placed side-by-side to form a table surface of needed area; some are pie-shaped wedges and fit together to form a round table.

BUNCHING TABLES

Bunk Bed A narrow bed, originally fastened to the wall, now available freestanding; double-decked with a small stepladder attached; the nautical aspect and space-saving size make bunk beds a practical choice for children's rooms.

BUNK BEDS

Burl Strong markings that emerge when wood is cut through a bole; caused by a large outside growth on a tree trunk, an abnormality that offers designers furniture veneers with unique patterns.

Burlap An open-weave fabric that resembles hopsacking; admired for its adaptability, countless colors, and extra-wide sizes which allow for room-width or picture-window drapery treatments without having to be seamed.

Butler Finish A soft lustrous matte finish on silver; hundreds of tiny scratch marks are incised (patterned after the almost invisible ones resulting from frequent polishing by the butler in one-time stately homes); this finish is an alternate choice to the brightly burnished effect preferred by some silversmiths.

Butler's Table Removable tray tops a folding stand; popularly used as an occasional table or small serving bar; mahogany and fruitwoods are traditional for eighteenth-century versions; present-day styles take advantage of materials like steel and lucite.

Butterfly Table A type of drop-leaf or gate-leg table whose supports are shaped like wings; a Colonial American piece.

BUTTERFLY TABLE

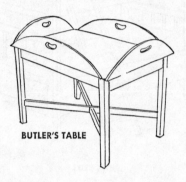

BUTLER'S TABLE

Butterfly Chair A chair constructed on a continuous metal frame that forms a base ending in a pair of wings at the top back; a one-piece sling seat made of canvas, plastic, or leather is stretched over the frame; first produced in 1938 by a team of industrial designers; also called a sling chair.

Button Tufting Seat and back cushions held firmly in place by fabric-covered buttons that are stitched through to the webbing; the tightly sewed buttons puff up the surrounding fabric, giving the upholstery a deeply quilted effect.

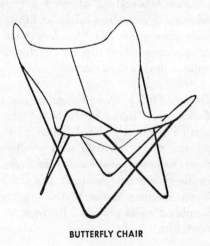

BUTTERFLY CHAIR

BUTTON-TUFTED CHAIR

32

C

Cabaña The Spanish word that has become synonymous with summer beaches; a portable fabric bathhouse or sun shelter; of striped canvas or bold solid colors.

Cabinetmaker A craftsman who designs and makes fine articles of wood furniture.

Cabochon A term borrowed from a gemstone shape; convex, polished but not faceted; usually oval; used on chair legs during the eighteenth century.

Cabriole Leg Furniture leg that curves in an S-shape, outward at the top, then inward and tapering down to the foot; widely used in the eighteenth century.

CABRIOLE LEG

Cache Pot Decorative porcelain, earthenware, or metal holder that conceals an ordinary red clay flowerpot.

CACHE POT

Café Curtains The name derives from the tiered-curtain arrangement used in French cafés and restaurants; tiers may be pulled aside individually to control light and air.

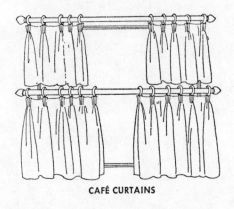

CAFÉ CURTAINS

CAMPAIGN CHEST

Camel-back Sofa The back is shaped with a high center curve, suggestive of a camel's hump; a style feature introduced by Chippendale; exaggerated versions appeared during Victorian times.

Camp Stool A folding metal frame with a canvas seat; very light and easy to carry; used by artists on sketching trips and by campers.

Canapé A French sofa of the Louis XVth period (the same word describes bits of toast with various cocktail spreads—the word itself means toast, therefore, the toast is a *seat* for caviar, pâté, or spreads).

CAMEL-BACK SOFA

Cameo Relief carving of a gem stone; the design is raised rather than incised; opposite of intaglio.

Campaign Chests Wood chests of drawers with brass-bound corners and recessed, brass drawer pulls; sometimes in sections so they can stack; originally made to carry army officers' equipment; of the eighteenth century; a variety of sizes and widths makes campaign chests practical for contemporary use.

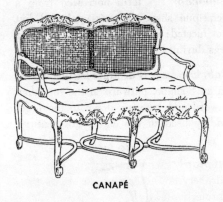

CANAPÉ

Candelabrum A decorative candle-holder with several extending arms or branches; silver, ormolu, vermeil, crystal, wrought iron are commonly used; plural, candelabra.

CANDELABRUM

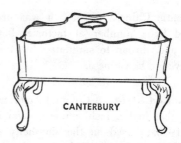

CANTERBURY

Cane Slender strips of bamboo or rattan woven into a flexible material for chair and sofa seats and backs, table tops under glass, headboards, etc. First brought into England from the Orient in the latter part of the seventeenth century, it has never lost popularity or attractiveness as a decorative material; it even lends its open-work pattern to screen-printed simulations on wallpaper and fabric.

Cantilever Construction An architectural principle by which a support is used at only one side of a structure; the technique is now applied to furniture; a chair appears to be set on just two legs—in reality, the legs which start in front continue in one curved shape to the back.

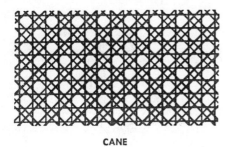

CANE

.CANTILEVER CONSTRUCTION

Canopy Wood framework with fabric drapery that tops a four-poster bed; any protective awning used outside a building.

Canterbury An occasional furniture piece made with partitions to hold magazines, sheet music, portfolios; wood or other materials used.

Canton China Also called export, China trade, terms used to describe the china brought by clipper ships to England and the United States during the eighteenth and nineteenth centuries; characteristic motifs were the lotus and other flowers, butterflies; monotone blue-and-white; the blue willow pattern of pagodas and bridges became almost synonymous with the ware; never an

35

authentic Chinese pattern, it was produced by a number of factories both here and abroad to simulate what they believed to be Chinese.

Cape Cod Style A Colonial American style that had a fashionable revival in the 1930s; based on the simplicity of the earliest American house—a compact, one-story-and-attic cottage; rustic pine and maple furniture: butterfly tables galore, Windsor chairs, braided rag rugs, patchwork quilts, primitive iron lamps and accessories, etc.

Capo di Monte Ware Porcelain made near Naples, Italy, in the eighteenth century; sculptured figurines, tureens, groups of storybook or historical personalities; very colorful and decorative.

Captain's Chair A spindle-back Windsor chair with taller than usual legs; said to be practical for a steamship captain on the bridge; popular for taverns and restaurants with nautical décor.

Carafe A glass water bottle; also a type of metal decanter made today with a heat/cold-retaining glass lining; a bedside or desk-top accessory.

Carlton House Desk One of Sheraton's noted designs in satinwood and mahogany, it is a practical working desk; a semicircular row of pigeonholes and compartments runs along back and sides, and a pierced brass gallery is often a decorative feature. Carlton House was the London home of George IV while he was Prince Regent.

Carnival Glass Called poor man's Tiffany and sometimes taffeta glass, this take-off of iridescent Tiffany glass was created as a premium or giveaway in the early 1900s; today it has become a collector's item.

Carpet vs. Rug Carpet is roll goods of continuous length; it is cut off to needed dimensions or used for wall-to-wall installation; rug always shows a wood or hard-surface flooring border all around; it is also woven to set sizes; has bound or fringed edges.

Cartouche An ornament extensively used since the seventeenth century; a flat shield-shaped plaque with curved, rolled ends; devised to hold an inscription or monogram; may be of stone when an architectural trim, or of wood when applied to furniture or paneling.

CARTOUCHE

Cartridge Pleating A type of drapery heading composed of tubular pleats filled with wadding; set in a clustered series, they resemble a cartridge belt.

Caryatid A sculptured female figure used as an architectural supporting column and as a furniture detail; in popu-

36

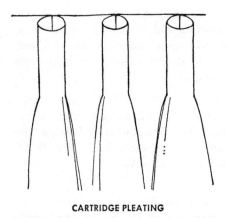

CARTRIDGE PLEATING

lar use during the classic revival of the early nineteenth century.

Case Goods The trade term for major wood furniture pieces—the large chests, buffets, breakfronts, etc.—as opposed to occasional furniture or upholstered pieces.

Cased Glass, or Overlay Two-color effects achieved by fusing a layer of red, green, blue, amber to clear glass; the pattern is then cut out through the colored areas to reveal the clear glass beneath; the technique is supposed to have originated in nineteenth-century Bohemia (Czechoslovakia), but there are evidences of sixteenth-century Venetian use of the process.

Casement Cloth Generic term for all kinds of sheer, lightweight curtain and drapery fabrics which may have unusual weaves (openwork stripes, hemstitched look, thick-and-thin yarns, etc.); made of all fibers and blends.

Casement Window A window that opens inward or outward from a vertical center opening; hinged; often set with small panes of glass; in use since Elizabethan times.

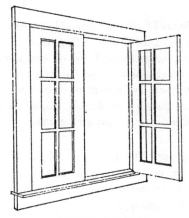

CASEMENT WINDOW

Caster 1) A container with a sifter top for salt, pepper, sugar; usually made of silver in a cylindrical shape; many were engraved or chased over total surface.
2) A small wood or metal wheel attached to furniture legs to provide easy mobility; an eighteenth-century invention.

CASTER

Cast-iron Furniture Very ornate, curlicued garden furniture of the Victorian periods; often painted deep green or white; a favored casting represented clusters of grapes and vine leaves; much more brittle than wrought iron.

Cathedral Ceiling A double-height or story-and-a-half-high ceiling that may follow the pointed lines of cathedral vaults when used in period-style architecture; or, as in contemporary usage, it may just be of double height with some unusual window arrangement.

Causeuse The French word for love seat or overscaled chair that is wide enough to accommodate two people; *causer* means to chat.

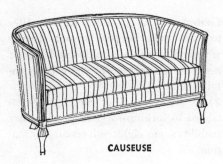

CAUSEUSE

Cedar Pink to reddish-brown color wood that darkens with age; smooth, close grain with many knots which release a distinctive aromatic odor that is moth repellent; the more knots, the stronger and more effective the scent; cedar is used mainly for linings in storage chests, closet interiors.

Celadon A soft, lovely shade of grayed green; first used as a glaze on Chinese porcelain and pottery; it became a favored background and paint color during the Georgian and Federal American periods.

Cellaret Small cabinet with doors; used for storing wine and liquor bottles, bar glassware; has a drawer for knives and utensils.

Center Guide A quality construction feature that makes drawers glide evenly without sticking; a strip of wood is glued to drawer opening and runs from front to back; a matching groove in the drawer bottom slides over this strip.

Centerpiece The center of attraction in a table setting; figurines, flowers, fruit, "polished" fresh vegetables, epergnes, candelabra, tureen, etc.; any imaginative arrangement that is tasteful; all elements except lighted candles are kept below eye level.

Chair Rail The top molding of a dado or wainscot; since its height is usually that of a side chair, it becomes a useful device to keep a chair back from marking the painted wall above.

Chaise Longue Literally, a "long" chair, *not* a "lounge" chair; a chair with an elongated seat or a daybed for resting or reclining; generally a boudoir piece, but contemporary interior designers frequently use a squared-off version placed at right angles at either side of a fireplace.

CHAISE LONGUE

Chaise Percée A seating piece, a nicety of the mid-eighteenth century and especially in French royal palaces; it was used to conceal and dignify the king's chamber pot; made of cane with a lift-up top it is still used today to hide the toilet unit and serve as an extra seating element in the bathroom.

Chandelier Lighting fixture suspended from the ceiling; many branched to hold a number of candles (antique) or light bulbs; styles vary from the very ornate with crystal prisms to simple wrought iron, rustic wagon wheel, and modern glass-globed versions.

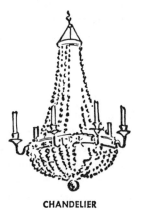

CHANDELIER

Chenille A fabric with a deep, soft, silky pile which resembles a caterpillar's fuzz; may be made of any fiber or combination; *chenille* is the French word for caterpillar.

Cherry A hard wood with a raylike grain; light pink-brown with wavy markings; good resistance to warping; popular for Early American period furniture; also used as veneer combined with other cabinet woods.

Chesterfield A fully upholstered, usually tufted, sofa simple and comfortable with a tailored, squarish look; named after the eighteenth-century notable, the Earl of Chesterfield.

Chestnut (wormy) A wood with coarse, open grain that looks like oak but is porous; frequent attacks by worms give it a characteristic texture; used mainly for concealed parts, low-cost country-style furniture, wall paneling where a timeworn, antique feeling is part of the scheme.

Cheval Glass A full-length, wood-framed, mirror, designed to swing back and forth to permit different viewing perspectives; set on four legs that are joined to a stretcher; simple or ornate; a cheval screen is similar, with tapestry or fabric instead of mirror, for use in front of a fireplace as a protective screen. (*Illustration page 40.*)

Chevron A V-shaped pattern applied as a separate trim; a fabric woven in a series of V's.

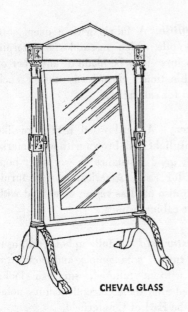

CHEVAL GLASS

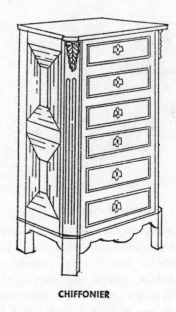

CHIFFONIER

Chiavari Chair Ladder-back with rush seat; usually painted black; a small inexpensive chair with general utility; serviceable in any style of informal room; made in Chiavari, Italy.

CHIAVARI CHAIR

Chiffonier A late eighteenth-century construction that combines chest and bookcase; also a tall narrow chest of drawers for odds and ends—the French word means collector of rags.

Chimney Piece The wood, stone, marble, or brick structure that surrounds a fireplace; simple or ornate depending upon the over-all architectural style of the room.

China Dogs Pottery figurines of different breeds of dogs have been popular since the mid-eighteenth century; among them, the brown-and-white toy spaniel with its gold leash, patterned after Charles II's favorite pet, is a typical example of Chelsea ware.

Chinese Rug A rug woven of silk yarn, with soft pale ground colors—ivory, rose, yellow, beige—that make it adaptable to most eighteenth-century interiors as well as to present-day decorative schemes; the pattern is woven in blue, which makes a Chinese rug immediately recognizable; motifs are interpretations of ancient religious sym-

40

bols and are concentrated at the four corners and the borders.

Chinoiserie A broad, all-inclusive term that describes many decorative furnishings taken from original Chinese sources; starting as a trend in the late seventeenth century, flourishing in the eighteenth, especially in France, and recently revived as the "Far East look" in contemporary decoration.

Chintz Plain-weave cotton of varying weights and qualities; protected by its high-gloss finish, chintz may be used for many decorative furnishings—bedspreads, draperies, slipcovers, tablecloths, etc.

Chintzy A slang expression for naive, inelegant decoration; not necessarily vulgar but affectedly proper.

Chipboard A material made of wood chips mixed with glue and molded under pressure; used for many kinds of mock wood decorative accessories where solid woods might be too costly or even too heavy; marketed under various trade names, such as Syrocowood.

Chippendale, Thomas (England, 1718–79) Probably the best-known and most widely imitated English cabinetmaker; the first craftsman to publish a text on design: *The Gentleman and Cabinet-Maker's Director*, 1754; he based many of his own creations on Chinese source material (this variation was called Chinese Chippendale); mahogany was his favored wood although much of

his furniture was fashionably lacquered or gilded, and other pieces were made to resemble bamboo; all stress ease, comfort, elegance. (*Illustration page 42.*)

Chromium Plating Furniture made of various metals is given a rust- and corrosion-resistant surface by an electroplated layer of chromium.

Claw-and-ball Foot A carved foot resembling a bird's or dragon's claw holding a ball; the terminal to a curved chair leg; widely used on English and American furniture of late seventeenth century and Georgian periods.

CLAW-AND-BALL FOOT

Clerestory, or Clearstory, Windows A series of low windows set high in a wall; most cathedrals and large churches use this type of upper window for lighting and ventilation—the pictorial stained-glass windows at the ground floor level being immovable; many contemporary architects find the clerestory arrangement an aid to privacy in residential buildings.

Cloisonné Varicolored enamels are poured into a pattern which has its design areas sectioned off by thin metal strips; one of the oldest methods of fin-

CHIPPENDALE DESIGNS

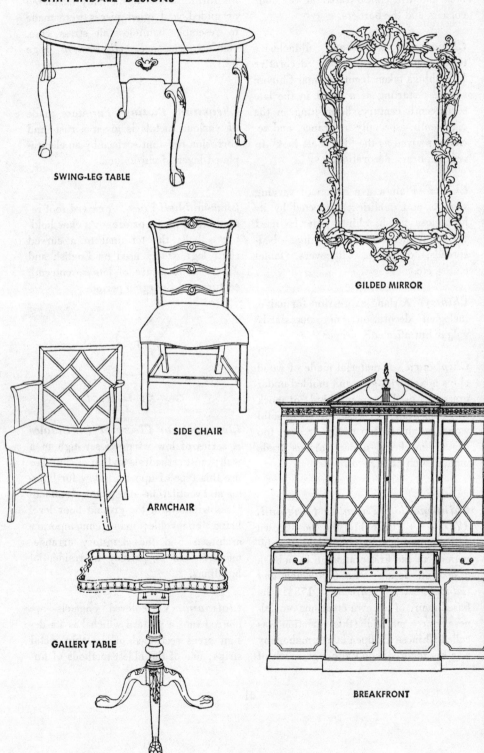

SWING-LEG TABLE

GILDED MIRROR

SIDE CHAIR

ARMCHAIR

GALLERY TABLE

BREAKFRONT

ishing for greater permanence; it is most often applied to small accessories like cigarette boxes, vases, ash trays, etc.

Coaster Originally a chased silver or cut crystal holder to take the drip from an opened wine bottle; today, coasters are small discs to be placed under individual drinking glasses to protect table surfaces from moisture; made of all imaginable materials from plastic to terry cloth as well as the traditional silver and crystal.

Cobbler's Bench A low seating piece, originally a Colonial workman's bench with compartments for tools and nails; more often used today as a cocktail table.

COBBLER'S BENCH

Collage A collage is an artistic montage of bits of paper, cloth, string, wire, and miscellaneous materials that are glued to canvas or cardboard; painters as noted as Picasso have created collages as an alternate form of expression; the French word for glue is *colle*.

Colonial American Period (1620–1780) From the time of the Pilgrims' arrival in 1620, the craftsmen in America began to develop distinctly native designs; in the beginning, they were plainly reminiscent of the Jacobean designs with which the settlers were familiar, but with availability of domestic pine and maple, a less weighty look gave the furniture its own character; as time went on, other cabinetmakers emigrated from England and design became more sophisticated, emulating prevailing English fashions but simplified and made adaptable to our different climate and room sizes; soon a distinctive regional style emerged—the "Philadelphia look," the "New England look," etc.

By the middle of the eighteenth century these specific American style innovations took their place in the Colonial household: the Governor Winthrop secretary/desk, the bonnet-topped highboy, the chest-on-chest—all henceforth to be classified as Colonial American. (*Illustration page 44.*)

Colonial American Rugs Rustic, informal braided rag rugs; oval and round; hooked styles with cut pile or uncut loops; black, brown, neutral colors are authentic since homemade dyes of the time were rarely bright.

Colorfast A term that describes materials whose color fades very little or not at all during its normal life span.

Color Schemes Combinations of colors selected for room decoration; they can be characterized as neutral, warm, cool, and low key. Neutral colors are beige, putty, gray, black, white—the sometimes muddy, "off" shades; warm schemes are dominantly red, orange,

COLONIAL AMERICAN PERIOD

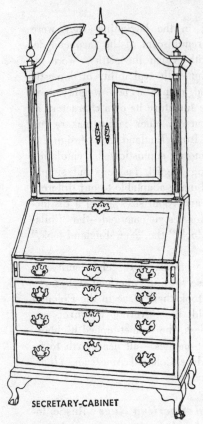

SECRETARY-CABINET

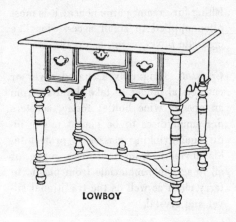

LOWBOY

SLANT-FRONT DESK

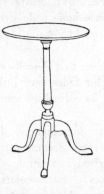

CANDLE TABLE

BRACE-BACK
WINDSOR ARMCHAIR

yellow—not necessarily in their pure strength, but more livably lightened to peach, pink, rose, lemon, and pale tints of mauve; cool schemes feature either blue or green, or a pleasing mixture of the two; low-key schemes are predicated on grayed colors and soft pastels—celadon green is a perfect example of low-key color.

Comb-back Chair A chair style developed in the mid-eighteenth century; an all-wood construction with a comb-like arrangement of rails and spindles; the center section of the back is tall, arms are on the same level as the sides and continue in a curve; over-all, a variation of the standard Windsor chair.

COMB-BACK CHAIR

Commode A chest of drawers; originally, this French word defined a small, bow-fronted chest of drawers set on curving legs; inlaid and often gilded; in Victorian times, both in England and the United States, the term referred particularly to a night stand or bedside table that concealed a chamber pot. (*See* Louis XIV.)

Complementary Colors These are colors placed opposite each other on the color wheel—red/green, blue/orange, violet/yellow; when mixed together each of these pairs produces a neutral gray shade.

Composition The pleasing arrangement of miscellaneous objects into an attractive and meaningful whole. A current method of selling flat silver or dinnerware; for example, forty-eight-piece service for eight, ninety-six-piece service for twelve, and so forth.

Compote A low bowl set on a footed or stemmed base; porcelain or glass, sometimes silver; used for serving fresh or cooked fruit, berries, candy, etc.; the word is French, meaning stewed fruit.

COMPOTE

Connecticut Chest A type of chest made in Connecticut, around Hartford, in the middle of the eighteenth century, with a deep blanket compartment in the top and two drawers below; characterized by low relief carving on the front. The upper section was usually divided into three parts containing the so-called sunflower and tulip motifs, actually believed to be the Tudor rose and the thistle; also similar, the Hadley chest.

Conservatory A glass-enclosed room, sun porch, or separate small greenhouse to grow plants and flowers year round; the traditional setting for many a Victorian proposal of marriage.

Console Table A wall table usually made with only two front legs and half round so that it may be permanently attached to the wall; often used in pairs in foyers and in period dining rooms to hold decorative vases or serving equipment. (*See* Hepplewhite.)

Contemporary American Rugs All styles and period designs are represented in current manufacture plus solid-color twist, shag, loop pile, embossed, velvet, etc.; patterns range from those inspired by historical material to the most avant-garde abstractions.

Contour Chair Molded to follow the contour of a human body and lessen fatigue through correct posture; of molded plywood (the Eames chair) or molded plastic (Eero Saarinen's pedestal).

Conversation Pit A square or rectangular sunken area in the floor, built to accommodate seating units and confine them to a reserved section; an experimental trend in contemporary architecture which suits the environment to social needs.

Co-ordinated Groups Furniture, floor coverings, fabrics, decorative accessories, etc. that have been planned to "go together" by their respective manufacturers; following a mutually agreed-upon fashion theme (for example, Far Eastern, Spanish), an appropriate color palette is adopted, and related design motifs are interpreted by all in varying proportions; special settings in stores assemble the theme merchandise into co-ordinated presentations making selection easier for the consumer.

Copenhagen Porcelain The Royal Copenhagen Porcelain Factory started production around 1760; it is still one of the great European style-setters; among its patterns is the famous *Flora Danica* service—every known botanical specimen is faithfully hand-painted, each flower on a different size plate; the original set is in Rosenborg Castle, but copies are in current manufacture.

Coquillage Ornamentation carved in the shape of a scallop shell; seen almost everywhere and on every possible object during the rococo period of the eighteenth century; the French word for shell is *coquille*.

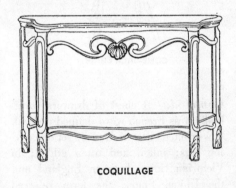

COQUILLAGE

Corduroy Cotton velvet with its pile in narrow or broad wales (stripes); its wide color ranges and widths make corduroy a practical fabric for bedspreads and throws, draperies, upholstery in formal and casual setting.

Corner Chair This pull-up chair has a right-angled back so that it can fit into a corner; arms are of the same height as back; a late seventeenth-century design.

CORNER CHAIR

Corner Cupboard Made with a triangular back able to be fitted into the room's corner; base is cabinet, upper section is shelved for china, books, etc.; with or without glass doors.

Cornice An ornamental strip, plain-edged or contoured, usually placed above draperies to conceal fixture and hardware; may be strip-lighted underneath to provide diffused lighting.

CORNICE

Cornucopia Classical symbol of plenty, the horn overflows with fruit or flowers; an ornamental detail.

Coromandel Screen Multiple-paneled, lacquered screen with scenic, floral, and figure motifs; although Chinese, its name is taken from the Coromandel coast of southern India from where these magnificent accessories were shipped on their long voyages to France and England during the late seventeenth century and afterward.

Cosy Corner A phenomenon of the 1890s—a hideaway within the living room; a corner unit, it was composed of right-angled, tufted velvet or plush banquettes; many gay pillows, hanging lighting fixture of Turkish style, Turkish bric-a-brac, even a few potted palms; also called a Turkish corner.

Court Cupboard A heavy oak buffet made of two open-back tiers separated by a somewhat clumsy, bulbous pair of uprights; for displaying silver, pewter; china; introduced in the fifteenth century, it was a standard household accessory by the seventeenth, then became outmoded.

Cove A curved, concave area that joins floor to wall, wall to ceiling, without apparent seams; cove lighting illuminates a room from behind a cornice placed at the ceiling cove; cove installation of hard-surface floor covering brings the material up from the floor to curve over baseboard in one smooth effect.

Crackleware China that has a network of tiny cracks over the glazed surface; first, an accident that was the result of faulty firing; then, since the effect was admired it was made a deliberate asset; it is also known as crazing.

Cranberry Glass Rich red glass popular in England and the United States since the 1880s; entire table services were fashioned as well as accessory items; sometimes combined with clear glass for contrast.

Crash All cotton or a blend of fibers; plain weave and crisp to the touch; takes well to prints; frequently the background is kept natural color or ecru.

Crazing, see Crackleware

Credenza The Italian word for a long narrow table used to display silver and other decorative accessories; originally, a fifteenth-century church table for holding ritual accessories, the credenza has become a storage piece more like a buffet than a table.

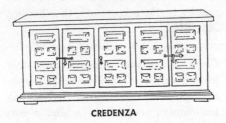

CREDENZA

Cretonne Plain weave, heavier than chintz or crash; mostly traditional eighteenth-century English patterns like trellises, huge bouquets, foliage.

Crewel Embroidery Wool yarn in a multitude of shades is worked on natural-ground linen; in the seventeenth century when it first became fashionable, it was primarily an upholstery material; today, a vast assortment of do-it-yourself kits offers a crewel-work pattern for practically every purpose—wall hanging, pillow top, pin cushion, etc.; and there are many more subjects besides the traditional leaf and flower patterns of old.

CREWEL EMBROIDERY PATTERN

Cricket Any small footstool set on short legs; it first was a kneeling stool for church use.

Crown Glass Flat glass blown so that it has a disklike bubble or bull's eye in the center; used in doors of high-quality breakfronts and cabinets; each section has an individual piece of glass set into a surrounding frame as opposed to one pane of glass behind a trellis of wood, as used in less expensive furniture.

Cruet A glass bottle for holding oil or vinegar; two are usually used together at the table; may be enclosed in a filigree silver holder for a more dressed-up look.

CRUET

Crystal Fine-quality clear glass that contains a large amount of lead and potash to give it greater weight, less brittleness, a resonant ring when tapped, and brilliant sparkle; ordinary table glass lacks these very particular features.

Cupid's Bow Carving An ornamental carving that made the top rail of chair backs; many Chippendale settees and chairs use this curving trim.

CUPID'S BOW CARVING

Currier & Ives The first and leading American lithographers of quantity prints from the 1830s to 1907; early black-and-white prints were hand-colored; later, the color-printing process was available and their seven thousand subjects took on realistic hues; about every aspect of American life from politics to prize fighting was interpreted; many of the smaller-scale drawings are still being used as pictorial subjects for greeting cards.

Curule Chair An ancient Roman backless bench seat set on X-shaped, curving legs; contemporary furniture designers have adapted the style to current use, in particular for dressing-table stools, foyer and entryway occasional pieces.

Custom-made Any product—from furniture to window shades—that is made to given specifications of size, color, price, etc.

Cut Glass A type of decorative glass very popular in the late nineteenth and

CUT GLASS PATTERN

49

early twentieth centuries for tableware and accessories; with over-all cutting in a wide variety of patterns—diamond shapes, stars, flowers, pineapples, and many others—brought rainbow sparkle to table top and china cabinet.

Cypress, (pecky) Soft wood with a compact, close grain; resembles satinwood; light beige to dark brown color; heavily textured surface; too soft for most uses other than wall paneling.

D E

D

Dado The lower section of a wall, it can be paneled in wood or painted; offers contrast to a wallpapered or fabric-covered top section.

Damascene Gold and silver wires inlaid into steel, copper, or bronze by hammering; a process invented by the goldsmiths of ancient Damascus; used for a variety of decorative objects such as boxes, trays; designs are usually traceries, arabesques.

Damask A fabric with woven pattern; resembles brocade but is flatter and lighter in weight; top surface is satiny and lustrous with the motifs standing out just slightly from the background; in all fibers.

Danish Modern Swedish or Scandinavian Modern—the terms are interchangeable and refer to one style; contemporary, simplified furniture and furnishings whose absence of ornamentation gives them an ageless, dateless character. (*Illustration page 54.*)

Dante Chair X-shaped legs which can be folded back are the feature of this chair that was in residential and public use during the Renaissance; based on ancient Greek and Roman styles, it was first made backless, then in the late sixteenth century a back was added for comfort; and, finally, upholstery softened its once all-wood construction, also called a Savonarola chair.

DANTE CHAIR

Davenport An American term for any style of sofa; a small, drawered desk

DANISH MODERN

STACKING STOOLS

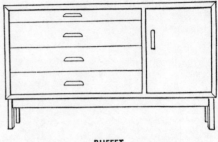

BUFFET

HANS WEGNER FOLDING CHAIR

HANS WEGNER CHAIR

with a slanting top that can be used as a writing table.

DAVENPORT DESK

Day Bed Already in use in Shakespeare's time, this single sofa bed has an adjustable headboard that can be slanted backward; each subsequent design period brought in some new variation of this versatile piece. (*See* Studio Couch.)

Decalcomania, or Decals Pictures and patterns are printed in reverse on thin paper or plastic; they are moistened and transferred to an object, rubbed in, and peeled away—the picture remains but the paper has gone; decals are used for decorating china and glassware; on china and pottery they are applied under the glaze to ensure permanence; also called transfers, the process is a short cut to achieving a hand-painted look at less cost, in less time.

Decanter A decorative glass or crystal bottle for holding wine or liquor after it has been poured from the original bottle; some are deeply cut in symbolic patterns: thistle, sheaf of wheat, vine leaves.

DECANTER

Decorative Motifs Symbols repeated, rediscovered, reinterpreted from antiquity to the present—throughout the world—and whenever an artisan has decided to put his individual touch to the fashions he has designed. The sun, moon, and stars; lion, eagle, dolphin, ram's head; shell, shield, trident, cornucopia, ribbon, Greek fret; flowers and plants (lotus, anthemion, palm, laurel, rose, bamboo, wheat sheaf, pomegran-

ate, acanthus leaf); monsters (sphinx, dragon, unicorn, phoenix, Medusa's head); these are found carved, printed, painted; as appliqués and inlays on furniture and furnishings.

Découpage Paper cutouts applied to various surfaces and later varnished for permanence; many home-fashion items have been decorated with these glued-on trimmings throughout the centuries—boxes, table tops, screens, etc.; the technique became especially important in times when austerity was a necessary watchword, since marble and other effects could be simulated via this method at much less cost than the genuine materials.

Delft Pottery made in Delft, Holland, since the middle of the seventeenth century; floral or scenic designs are usually painted in blue on a bluish-white ground, but there are examples of wine-color monotone effects and some multicolored treatments as well. The characteristic bluishness is caused by the special tin glazes used.

Della Robbia A family of artists and sculptors in Renaissance Florence; their decorative style is recognized by its wreaths, medallions, fruit and flower borders, portrait heads—all highly glazed in brilliant colors and almost three-dimensional in relief. (*Illustration page 56.*)

Diaper Pattern An age-old, diamond-shaped geometric design used as a small allover carving on wood, as a fabric print, or as a border trim.

55

DELLA ROBBIA

DIRECTOR'S CHAIR

Dinnerware The all-inclusive term for the plates and dishes that make up a table setting; they may be china, plastic, pottery, glass, or of any other material; dinnerware is a more accurate expression than china because of the assortment of possible materials.

Directoire Period (France, 1795–1804) A decorative style that retained many of the established Louis XVIth details while adding others inspired by objects Napoleon brought home from his campaigns in Egypt; the lion's head, sphinx, lyre were some of the motifs; colors grew richer and deeper; fruitwoods became increasingly popular as did ormolu trims on furniture.

Director's Chair The now legendary movie director's lightweight, folding armchair; canvas sling back and seat; X-shaped wood or metal frame; inexpensive unless leather-covered.

Distressed Finish This term was first used to describe well-worn wood furniture when it had aged naturally; it is used today as a man-made finish that simulates aging.

Divan A low sofa constructed like a Hollywood bed except that it is completely upholstered in a decorative fabric; the word is Turkish.

Documentary Pattern An adaptation or an exact copy of an earlier design; usually derived from a wallpaper or fabric of a past era.

Dolphin A motif used as ornament on furniture; an architectural detail on fountains, etc.

DOLPHIN MOTIF

DIRECTOIRE PERIOD

SIDE CHAIR

DROP-FRONT WRITING DESK

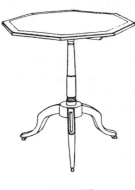

TEA TABLE

WIDE ARMCHAIR

Dormer Window A window set into a gable that projects outward from a slanting roof; an attic window.

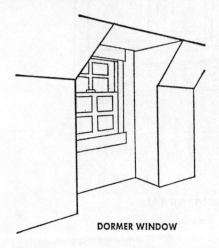

DORMER WINDOW

Double- (also Triple-) dome Top Bookcases or cabinets with wooden doors that are rounded off at the top; a popular construction for contemporary case furniture.

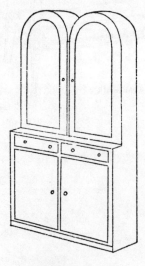

DOUBLE-DOME TOP

Double (also Triple) Dresser Two or three matching chests of drawers are joined into one piece that offers twice the amount of storage space as the average dresser; sold with or without a matching mirror.

Dovetail Construction A method of joining wood furniture parts without nails or metal; alternating wedge-shaped notches in the two pieces interlock and fit together tightly.

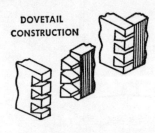

DOVETAIL CONSTRUCTION

Dowel A round hardwood peg that fits into a corresponding hole; a technique of joining furniture legs to stretchers, shelves to side walls, etc.

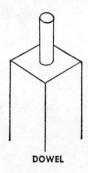

DOWEL

Down Soft fluff from the breast of goose or duck; regarded as the most luxurious filler for sofa cushions, bed pillows; since it has little resilience it is often combined with feathers for greater spring.

Dresden China Popular name for Meissen porcelain; figurines and flat serving dishes, lacy costumed ballerinas, shepherdesses, and romantic twosomes in pastoral settings are typical subjects found in this brightly glazed, hand-painted ware.

Drop Handle Also called a tear drop, a pendant handle that hangs from a metal plate attached to a drawer; popular pull from about 1690 through 1720.

DROP HANDLE

Drop-in, or Slip, Seat A removable, upholstered chair seat used mainly on side or dining-room chairs; an early eighteenth-century innovation still popular.

Drop-leaf Table A table with hinged leaves at the sides that can be lifted and are supported by additional legs or swinging sections; butterfly, gate-leg, and Pembroke styles.

Drop Repeat The printed motifs on a wallpaper or fabric placed so that they descend in diagonal direction instead of matching across the width.

DROP REPEAT MOTIF

Drum Table A round occasional table with a deep apron, small drawers all around; set on a pedestal base; sometimes leather-topped.

DRUM TABLE

Dry Sink Commonly used in nineteenth-century kitchens, a wooden cabinet with tin or copper well for dishwashing; frequently used now as a stand for potted plants or to hold bar equipment.

59

Dual-purpose Furniture Furniture designed to serve more than one purpose; e.g., a desk with drop leaves that convert it into a dining table; any sofa that opens into a bed, etc.

Duchesse Two armchairs plus a matching square bench that can be assembled to create a flexible chaise longue or day bed; the chairs face each other with the bench between them.

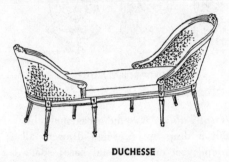

DUCHESSE

Duck A linen or cotton fabric similar to canvas and as durable; used for both indoor and outdoor slipcovers and upholstery.

Dumbwaiter, or Tier, Table Three graduated wooden trays attached to a center pedestal; the bottom tier has drawers fitted to hold flat silver; early eighteenth-century style popular in Colonial America and in England.

Dust Ruffle A floor-length, permanent ruffle placed over boxspring and under mattress and bed linen; made in shirred, box-pleated, or inverted corner-pleat styles; a coverlet spread is used to complete the ensemble; coverlet may match or contrast with the dust ruffle.

Dynasty A family or group that maintains rulership during successive generations; describes the many such periods in China from the pre-Christian era to the early twentieth century; for example, the Ming Dynasty lasted from 1368–1644; the Manchu from 1644–1912; after this the Chinese Republic succeeded the imperial dynasties; each dynasty identified the design characteristics of its time span, and each produced its unique style; the Ming Dynasty is probably the best known because of its influence on color and form.

E

Eames Chair The prototype of the body-contoured, molded plywood or plastic chair launched by American designer Charles Eames in 1939; the concept has had immeasurable influence on other contemporary furniture designs.

EAMES CHAIR

Ébéniste The French word for cabinetmaker is derived from *ébène*, meaning ebony; a worker in ebony signified a master craftsman; since ebony was a rare and precious wood, only a superlative artisan would dare to carve it.

Ebonizing Simulation of ebony by means of dull black paint, whenever genuine ebony was too costly or unavailable.

Ebony, Macassar Black or dark brown wood with lighter streaks; very smooth fine grain with heavy oil content; used particularly for inlays, decoration, framework.

Eclecticism A term applied today to a style of decoration in which furniture and accessories from past and present, from East and West, are gracefully and harmoniously combined.

Edwardian Period (England, 1900 —First World War) After Edward VII ascended the throne, the expected reaction to Victorianism in all its aspects emerged; decoration saw the revival of Louis XVth court styles now manufactured commercially with new, improved mechanical methods, and thus available to everybody; *Art Nouveau* innovations flourished: The brass bed, the glass vitrine for displaying cut glass and other bric-a-brac, the sets of gilded side chairs, and "suites" of upholstered pieces set the scene for most well-to-do middle-class homes; favored colors were old rose, ashes of roses, Copenhagen blue, dark green, deep red, with cream, ivory, and pale gray the best-liked wall colors.

Egg and Dart A border decoration alternating egg-shaped and arrowhead motifs in stone, metal, and wood; used profusely on furniture and as an architectural trim since the Middle Ages.

EGG AND DART

Egg Shell The thinnest possible porcelain, which originated in China; typical of Belleek china and some Minton.

Egyptian Style Just as the word *chinoiserie* defines Far Eastern design origins, the Egyptian style characterizes early French Empire symbols: the lotus-topped capital, sphinx, lion's head, etc. that appeared mainly as ormolu trim on furniture.

Elevation An interior designer's scale drawing or water-color sketch of sections of a room; shows the placement of windows, doors, other architectural details.

Elizabethan Period (England, 1558–1600) Italian styles dominated the decorative scene in the reign of Elizabethan I just as Italian themes did in Shakespeare's plays; furniture began to

EGYPTIAN-STYLE ARMCHAIR

link utility with decoration; legs and supporting posts became huge, bulbous, and ornately carved; mirrors were introduced at this time as wall accessories; suites of chairs appeared, setting a trend for some three hundred years to come; many previously unexplored woods were used, besides massive oak; leather upholstery became fashionable; nail-studded trim seemed to remain as a memento of the great Spanish Armada's defeat; overscale hand-loomed tapestries gave color and interest to large, otherwise empty, wall areas.

Elm A hardwood ranging in color from pale to dark red-brown; grain resembles oak; elm is easy to work into curves; its burls create decorative veneers for all types of furniture.

62

Embedment The technique of enclosing a variety of unexpected articles—from coins to dried grasses, paper clips to sea horses—in a block of clear plastic; used for paperweights, serving trays, other decorative accessories.

Embossing Designs that are molded or carved in relief; usually worked from the inner side of the object. (*See* Repoussé.)

Empire Period (France, 1804–15) Napoleon proclaimed himself the first Emperor of France and a new style emerged in celebration; emphasis was on decorative elements that related to the new monarch's exploits or those that flattered him—the letter "N," the laurel wreath (triumphant symbol of ancient Rome), a glorified bee, the sphinx and other reminders of the North African campaigns; colors became regal with rich dark green, violet, plum, ruby, black; heavy woods like ebony and mahogany, trimmed with elaborate brass and ormolu details accompanied the emphatic colors; satin stripes, small-scaled damasks were generally favored; crisp thin cottons, gauzy weaves offered relief to the sometimes overpowering weight of furniture and upholstery.

EMPIRE PERIOD

CHEST

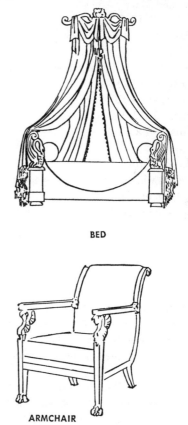

BED

ARMCHAIR

Engine Turning A special treatment is applied to metal objects; fluting, crisscrossing, geometric borders are produced on lathes; generally used as finish on silver cigarette boxes and cases, table lighters, powder boxes, and other decorative metal pieces.

English Period Styles by dates
Gothic fourteenth and fifteenth centuries
Tudor 1500–58
Elizabethan 1558–1600
Jacobean 1600–40
Puritan 1640–60
Charles II 1660–90
William and Mary 1690–1702
Queen Anne 1702–20
Georgian 1720–1800 (George I, II, and III)
Regency 1800–20 (Prince Regent, later King George IV)
Pre-Victorian 1820–37
Victorian 1837–1900
Edwardian 1900–14

Envelope Table A small, compact card table which has four triangular hinged flaps on the top that open out to make it large enough for four people to sit at it comfortably.

Épergne A table centerpiece made of metal, crystal, or a combination of materials; small dishes or bowls are set on arms that branch out from a center pedestal; to serve fruit, cakes, nuts, etc.; designs may be very elaborate, especially those of the Victorian period.

Escritoire The French word for desk or small secretary; a let-down front forms the writing surface; pigeonholes and small drawers surmount a full chest-of-drawers base.

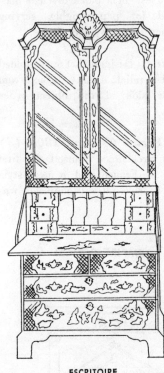

ESCRITOIRE

Escutcheon A small brass or other metal ornamental shield that surrounds a keyhole or backs a drawer pull on a piece of furniture or a door; in heraldry, the shield-shaped surface on which armorial bearings are displayed.

Étagère An open-shelved stand for displaying decorative objects; also called a whatnot; although of eighteenth-century origin it became identified with Victorian times; present-day styles combine steel, glass, and plastic to achieve a light, airy look.

ESCUTCHEON

Etched Glass Delicate frosted traceries of pattern on glass; motifs are created by application of acid to sections of glass not covered over with a wax that resists the bite of acid; used for all sorts of table glassware.

Etching A drawing scratched into a metal plate, inked, and transferred to paper; etchings are considered original art because the artist makes his own reproductions, numbers and signs each proof, and finally destroys the plate.

Extension Table Generally, for dining-room use, but any table which can be expanded by the addition of leaves inserted to form one uniform, larger surface.

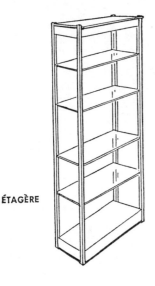

ÉTAGÈRE

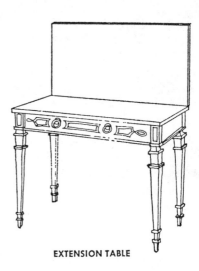

EXTENSION TABLE

F G

F

Faïence Fine earthenware, tin or metallic glazed; brightly colored decorations are applied over the glaze and after the first firing; the name derives from Faenza, the Italian city which produced much of this ware during the Renaissance; in Italy it is called majolica; in Holland, a similar technique of glazing and decoration is used on Delft pottery.

Family Room Peculiarly American in origin (the 1950s), a room singled out for "family interests"; often built adjacent to garage or kitchen; decorated in less formal style than living room and planned for home entertainment, TV watching, games, bar equipment.

Fanlight Semicircular or fan-shaped ornamental window placed above entrance door or French window; its metal ribs resemble radiating spokes of an opened fan.

Fauteuil A French armchair style; arms are open and may have a small

FANLIGHT

upholstered pad for resting the elbow; back and seat are upholstered; Louis XV and XVI periods. (*See* Louis XVI.)

Federal American Period (1780–1830) The name given to styles appearing after the establishment of the federal government in 1789; the first national symbol—our American eagle—made its initial appearance on all forms of furniture and furnishings and in every known material; otherwise, this style had an international look; Duncan Phyfe was influenced by French Empire

69

styles; Hitchcock's stenciled trim on black grounds has an English Regency overtone, and so forth; in rural sections of the United States, the design might be called regional—the Far West and Southwest exhibiting definite Spanish and Mexican characteristics; settlers in western Pennsylvania brought their colorful peasant crafts from Germany and Switzerland to found a new style, etc.

Felt A non-woven fabric made by compressing natural or synthetic fibers under heat; its cut edge can be used without hemming—it cannot ravel; made in extra-wide dimensions and available in broad color ranges; felt is decorative and appropriate for table covers, bedspreads, wall coverings, etc.; excellent material for glue-on or appliqué trims.

Fender Contoured metal guard rail placed in front of an open fireplace to keep logs and embers from rolling out.

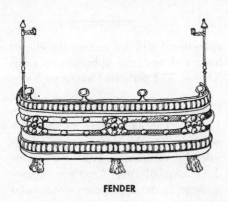

FENDER

Fenestration The arrangement of windows in a building.

Festoon A carved garland, swag, or drapery that is used as an applied trim on furniture; when made of fabric, it is used as an elaborate overdrapery.

FESTOON

Fiasco A long-necked wine bottle covered partially with braided straw or wicker. Generally, Tuscan Chianti is packaged this way; the bottles when empty make casual holders for wild flower bouquets, etc.; *fiasco* is Italian for flask.

Fiberglass Fabric made of finely spun glass threads; flame resistant, stable (does not shrink or sag), therefore suitable for draperies and curtains.

Fiddleback The violin-shaped center splat of a chair back, a characteristic of Queen Anne-style side chairs.

Figure-8 Chair Back Although the style originated in Venice during the eighteenth century, it is basically Queen Anne in mood; a ribbonlike figure 8 forms the back splat; combines well with today's contemporary furniture.

FEDERAL AMERICAN PERIOD

LADDER-BACK CHAIR

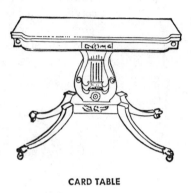

CARD TABLE

BULL'S-EYE MIRROR

BACHELOR'S CHEST

HITCHCOCK CHAIR

FIGURE-8 CHAIR BACK

Finial A decorative projection (ball, flame tip, pineapple, urn, etc.) which serves as a handle as well as a finishing trim; the center motif of a bonnet-top carving on a highboy or secretary; an ornamental way of fastening a lamp shade in place; as a knob on sugar bowl or teapot, etc.

FINIAL

Filigree Openwork patterns in metal, wood, twisted gold, or silver wire; filigree galleries edge period-style occasional tables; make decorative holders for glass cruets, ordinary condiment bottles, etc.

Fir Pale ivory-yellow wood with some of the same features as pine; used for inexpensive unfinished furniture, some concealed sections.

Fleur-de-lis, or -lys A stylized version of the three-petaled garden iris, this historic device has been the armorial symbol of the kings of France; as a decorative motif on fabric, wallpaper, china, it has been in use for hundreds of years; *lis* is French for lily.

FILIGREE GALLERY

FLEUR-DE-LIS

72

Flocking A method of applying loose, finely cut fibers to wallpaper or fabric in order to create a raised velvetlike pattern; the base material may be the same color as the flocking or in contrast to it.

Flokati Rug Shaggy wool area rug made in Greece; it is available in solid colors as well as in its natural off-white shade.

Floor Lamps Tall lamps traditional and contemporary in style, they radiate light across large areas; *bridge* lamp has an extension arm that can swing in any direction to focus light where needed; *reflector* types have a white glass bowl to shield the three-power bulb fitting; *pole* types have several directional spotlights arranged at intervals.

Fluffing Newly installed carpet has a tendency to fuzz or fluff; this is the result of short ends working their way up to the surface; they are not loose tufts; they disappear after cleaning and use.

Fluorescent Light Cool glareless light available in different tones including a rosy look; light is produced by passing an electric current through a gas enclosed in glass tubing; twice as much light is given and tubes last from three to six times longer than incandescent light bulbs.

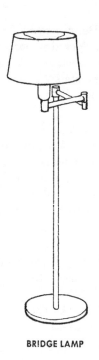

BRIDGE LAMP

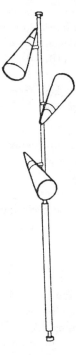

POLE LAMP

Flush Base Furniture that is level with the floor and constructed without legs.

Fondue Set A currently popular word for the chafing dish; fondue is a melted cheese concoction, prepared at the table and kept hot in a metal pan set upon an alcohol burner; the set is composed of the chafing dish and six or eight two-tined forks.

Formica Various laminated plastic sheets (melamine and phenolic materials); rigid enough for counter and table tops, wall paneling; all colors and simulated wood veneer patterns.

Fortuny Print A method of printing woven cotton fabric so that it resembles brocade and damask; perfected by Mariano Fortuny (1871–1949), whose Venetian factory is still in operation; most patterns are taken from documentary and antique sources.

Four-poster, or Tester, Bed A bed with a tall post at each corner to support a canopy; side curtains were closed at night to protect against cold and draft; today, the enclosing curtains are usually drawn back and fastened to the posts with tiebacks, there merely to preserve some decorative faithfulness.

Franklin Stove It really *was* invented by Ben Franklin! A cast iron stove with an opening like a fireplace that used wood fuel; today, it is a collector's item and still serviceable.

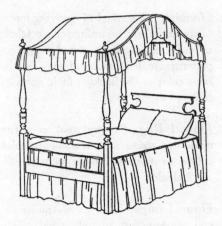

FOUR-POSTER BED WITH CANOPY

Freestanding As opposed to wall-hung or built-in furniture units, freestanding describes any piece which stands on its own base or feet.

French Door (also, French Window) A door that opens out onto a terrace or porch; its full-length vertical glass panels are set in pairs; often curtained with sheer fabric or pull-up blinds.

French Period Rugs Aubusson and Savonnerie styles are very similar—both are silky, soft, with carved pile outlining individual motifs; pastel colors; designs include arabesques, florals, urns, medallions, antique symbols.

French Period Styles by dates
High Renaissance 1500–1600
Baroque 1600–50
Louis XIV 1643–1715
Régence 1715–23
Louis XV 1723–74

Louis XVI 1774–93
Directoire 1795–1804
Empire 1804–15
Bourbon Restoration 1815–48
Second Republic 1848–52
Second Empire 1852–70
Art Nouveau 1890–1910 (*la belle époque*)

French Provincial Not a period but rather a term that defines a wide range of major French styles of the seventeenth and eighteenth centuries simplified into rustic or countrified versions; less formal and ornate than court pieces of the same dates: rush seating, for example, instead of luxurious silk

FRENCH PROVINCIAL STYLES

ARMOIRE

TABLE

ARMCHAIR

upholstery; fruitwoods were popular; metal hardware important; fabrics included small, subtly colored plaids, florals, toile de Jouy cottons; today's replicas of these furniture styles add distressed finishes to lend the look of authentic antiques.

Fresco Painting that is applied directly to a wet plaster wall surface; Michelangelo's ceiling paintings in the Sistine Chapel and Da Vinci's "Last Supper" are world-renowned examples of fresco decoration; (Italian for fresh).

Fretwork Pierced wood carvings used as a gallery or frieze on tables, for decoration on headboards, chair backs, etc., derived from Chinese furniture styles and particularly favored by Chippendale in the eighteenth century.

FRETWORK

Frieze 1) a band of carving between wall and ceiling; the effect often achieved with a wallpaper border; 2) any upholstery fabric with an uncut loop pile that may be a little harsh or rough to the hand (this version of the word is pronounced "free-zay").

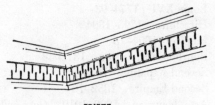

FRIEZE

Fruitwood Wood from fruit-bearing trees: pear, apple, cherry, etc.; all are firm, smooth textured; used mainly for fine veneers, inlays, and marquetry.

Functional Furniture Design styles which concentrate on purpose and usefulness rather than ornamentation; a Parsons table, for example, is purely functional—its beauty lies in its fulfillment of purpose.

Furniture Woods These are divided into two classifications: *hardwood* (trees with broad flat leaves) and *softwood* (evergreen or coniferous trees with needlelike leaves); hardwoods are less likely to split and splinter, have intricate grains and patterns; softwoods, such as fir, cedar, pine, and others are easily dented, and take well to paint and varnish finishes.

G

Gadroon Edge A curving, fluted border trim on furniture; although more usually associated with silver trays and hollow ware where it is used liberally as a finishing touch; known since Elizabethan times.

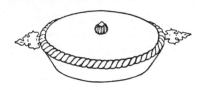

GADROON EDGE

Gallery As a furniture trim it is a pierced metal or wood railing that goes along the top edge of a table (*see* Chippendale); in architecture, a long hall that is used to display pictures and paintings; a central area from which other rooms open.

Game, or Gaming, Table A type of table in use from the early eighteenth century up to the present; its top may be hinged to fold back; usually has chessboard inlay; sometimes with can-dleholders at each corner and wells for chips added for period-style authenticity; when it has a backgammon layout, it is called a *trictrac* table after the French word for the game.

GAME TABLE

Gate-leg Table A variation of the drop-leaf table with two sets of legs that swing out like gates to support the raised leaves. (*See* William and Mary.)

Gazebo A pavilion, summerhouse, or domed garden shelter; often octagonal in shape, and sometimes screened-in all around.

Geode A rock formation with decorative effectiveness; quartz, rock crystal, amethyst, agate, jasper—semiprecious objects for collections, for display in étagères, etc.

Geometric Pattern Fabric, wallpaper, or carpet patterns that take their inspiration from basic geometric shapes: squares, rectangles, circles, triangles, octagons, etc.; many times these patterns are small scaled and deliberately kept to a simple color palette.

GEOMETRIC PATTERN

Georgian Periods (England, 1715–1800) Truly the golden age of design and decoration. The periods that spanned the reigns of the English Kings George I–III; the Georgian periods witnessed the rise of architecture as a profession; the advent of the city planner; furniture and furnishings were influenced by many concurrent events such as the popularity of rococo in France; Chinese designs brought back by the East India Company traders and the neo-classicism awakened by the excavations at Herculaneum and Pompeii; cabinetmakers flourished in all countries and began to develop recognizable personal styles. Every type of material was employed: silver, crystal, marble, native and exotic woods, metals; many different kinds of weaves and textures for the first time were created to fulfill particular purposes; many trends were still being set by continuing discoveries in the Far East; small refinements such as place settings of china and silver, fire screens, dressing tables, desk and other decorative accessories came into more general use.

Gesso A substance made of plaster of Paris or gypsum and glue; used for modeling ornamental trims which are applied to another surface and painted over or gilded such as picture and mirror frames, fireplace and ceiling moldings, wall paneling, etc.

Gibbons, Grinling (1648–1720) Innovative wood carver who arrived on the London scene in the late seventeenth century; he became an associate of the famed architect Sir Christopher Wren and created many of the carved fruit, foliage, and festoon motifs for Wren's buildings; was appointed Master Wood Carver to King George I in 1714.

Gimp A decorative braid that conceals the structural tacks and nails on upholstered furniture.

Girandole Wall sconce that is custom-

GEORGIAN PERIOD

BLOCK FRONT

ARMCHAIR

CABINET

HUNTBOARD

arily carved and gilded; it may have a small mirror inset behind the candle-holders.

Glass Blocks Strong thick blocks of textured glass are used like structural bricks for entire walls as well as for interior room dividers; they provide light while screening out an ugly view; curtains and blinds are not needed for privacy.

Glassware Table glassware is classified as: *stemware*—fashioned with bowl set on stem and base; *tumblers*—no base, at most a very low foot; *sham bottomed*—bar glassware with exaggeratedly thick bases suggesting a greater fluid capacity than is actual; stemware includes goblets, all varieties of wine, cocktail, and cordial glasses; tumblers include water glasses, juice glasses, highball, and iced beverage sizes; sham-bottomed ware includes shot glasses, measuring jiggers, single and double old-fashioned glasses.

Glaze In ceramics, the thin glossy coating that is fired on a clay body giving a hard non-porous impenetrable finish; on fabric, it is a finish that adds glossiness and stiffness (glazed chintz, glazed cotton satin).

Gobelins Tapestry Hand-woven tapestries made at the Gobelins works in Paris; since its founding in the seventeenth century the factory has employed artists of note to design its huge scenic and pictorial canvases; many of the subjects were mythological, allegorical, or purely narrative and romantic in content; contemporary designs have been created by painters as renowned as Marc Chagall, Henri Matisse, Jean Arp, Vasarely, and others.

Gooseneck Lamp A contemporary type of desk or utility lamp with a shaded globe set on a flexible metal column; it can be turned, raised, lowered, redirecting light in any direction.

Gothic Period Broadly, the span between 1100 and 1500; the Gothic was the age of the vast cathedral; design characteristics were tracery work, the trefoil, quatrefoil motifs, clustered columns, the pointed arch, linen-fold carving. It is understandable that the furnishings of the period reflected the architectural attitude; oak was the available wood and it was heavily carved and embellished; left mainly unpolished. Chests with lift-up tops, the canopied bed with its freestanding columns, folding chairs, long trestle tables with backless benches, iron hardware and bandings for trim—these are characteristic of the period.

GOTHIC CHEST

80

GOTHIC CUPBOARD

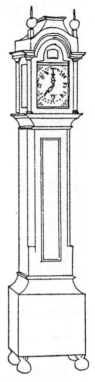

GRANDFATHER CLOCK

Governor Winthrop Desk A desk with a glass-doored upper cabinet, a three- or four-drawer base, and a fall-front slanting panel; when opened as a writing surface, the panel rests on concealed slides.

Grandfather, or Long, Clock A tall (6½ to 7 feet) wood-encased pendulum clock with weights and chimes; first designed in England toward the end of the seventeenth century; profusely trimmed with appliqués, veneers, scene paintings, marquetry, lacquer, etc.; these clocks reflected the furniture styles of their respective periods, i.e., Chippendale, Hepplewhite, Sheraton, and others; a shorter version (less than 6 feet high) is logically called a grandmother clock.

Graphics An all-encompassing term that describes most reproductions of art works such as engravings, etchings, woodcuts, lithographs, serigraphs, etc.; the value is determined by the artist's repute, the number of proofs pulled from the original plate, and the condition of these proofs.

Grass Cloth Woven dried grasses and reeds are glued to paper or fabric for wall coverings; wide variety of colors and weaves.

Greek Key, or Greek Fret An ornamental border made up of continuous interlocking geometric figures; some are square, others wave-shaped; in architecture, on fabric, as a rug border, on china.

GREEK KEY BORDER

Grille Metal screening made in a number of patterns (crisscross, geometric, Moroccan and Spanish wrought

GRILLE

iron, etc.) ; for use as room dividers, as doors on breakfronts and bookcases; sometimes the grille is lined with sheer, softly shirred fabric.

Grisaille Shades of gray in a mural painting; often used as an over-door decoration or ceiling fresco; a favorite Adam brothers' touch.

Gros Point A needlepoint stitch worked on canvas that has from ten to fourteen meshes per inch; suitable for chair seats, sofa pillows, wall hangings; *petit point* has from eighteen to twenty-four meshes per inch, is very fine, and best suited to be worked as pictures, miniatures, or for tiny details within a *gros point* tapestry.

Ground Color The background color of fabric, carpet, wallpaper, china, etc., on which all other colors are overprinted.

Guéridon A small occasional table, originally a holder for candelabra or decorative objects; named for a gaily dressed, turbaned Moorish galley slave called Guéridon, whose likeness was the supporting pedestal for a serving tray.

Guernsey Jug Small, plump jug made of silver, pewter, or other metal; with a raffia-wrapped handle and a knobbed lid; specifically used for serving hot liquids.

Gumwood A wood with pale pink-brown tone and attractive markings on a smooth even grain; a tendency to warp is corrected with plywood construction; softer than maple or birch, but its uses are similar—legs, stretchers, other exposed parts; combines well with mahogany and walnut because it can be stained to simulate them; such uses must be labeled "gumwood" to alert the purchaser to the fact that the object is neither walnut nor mahogany.

H I

H

Hadley Chest A Colonial storage chest made in Hadley, Massachusetts, from about 1675 to 1750; usually with a lift-up top and one or two drawers; the entire surface is decorated with motifs carved in low relief; also similar, the Connecticut chest.

Half-tester Bed A poster bed with only two back posts instead of four to support an abbreviated tester or canopy; often this may extend only about twelve inches from the back wall.

Hallmark An engraved mark traditionally used in England to stamp gold and silver objects that meet certain established quality standards; designer, maker, and date of the articles are also identified by their individual marks and symbols.

Hand Generally, a trade term that describes the "feel" of a fabric to the touch—softness, harshness, stiffness, suppleness, silkiness, resilience, etc.

Handkerchief Table A drop-leaf style with a triangular top and one triangular leaf which, when lifted, turns the top into a square table.

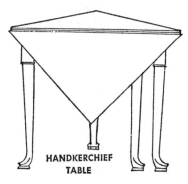

HANDKERCHIEF
TABLE

Hard-surface Floor Coverings Generic term for all floor coverings that are made of non-fibrous materials—vinyl, rubber, asphalt tile, cork, terrazzo, linoleum, ceramic tile.

Harlequin Pattern A print design derived from the patterned tights worn by the famous *commedia dell'arte* character Harlequin; it is an arrangement of

87

multicolor diamond shapes; used on chintz, sateen, other lightweight drapery fabrics, wallpaper.

Hassock An overstuffed, low cushion without legs used as a footstool or for extra seating; some are made with hinged, lift-up tops and can be used for storage.

Hat Stand A bentwood pole topped by a cluster of curved wooden hooks; a nineteenth-century convenience used in hallways, public lobbies, restaurants, also was made with a tubular base to hold umbrellas.

HAT STAND

Headboard Wood, fabric-covered, cane, or plastic panel at the head of a

bed; in all period and contemporary styles.

Hepplewhite, George (England, ?–1786) A trend-setting English cabinetmaker of the eighteenth century; like his colleague Chippendale, he prepared a sketchbook of original designs: *The Cabinet Maker and Upholsterer's Guide,* which was published after his death; the graceful Hepplewhite style features the shield-back chair, fluted legs, the sideboard as an integral part of the dining-room scene; veneers and painted finishes are also typical; many of his upholstered pieces derive from contemporaneous French fashions; today, furniture manufacturers are still producing excellent copies of Hepplewhite side chairs and dining-room sideboards.

Hibachi A portable, charcoal-burning iron cooker made in Japan; it may be brought to the table or used as an outdoor grill.

HIBACHI

Hickory A native American wood that not only looks like walnut but shares its qualities: hard, dense, adaptable.

High Riser Dual-purpose sleep sofa constructed so that its second spring

HEPPLEWHITE DESIGNS

SHIELD-BACK CHAIR

POUDREUSE

SIDEBOARD

TABLE

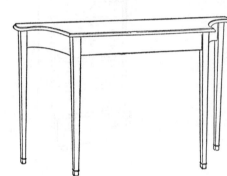

BOW-FRONT CHEST

SOFA

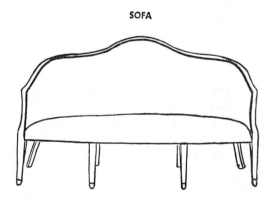

and mattress are concealed below the top set; when pulled out, they rise to the height of the upper unit by means of a lever; the two units may be set side-by-side or separated to form twin beds.

Highboy A two-sectioned chest of drawers; the base may be flush to the floor or set on feet; the top is usually bonneted; in contemporary design, the top is squared off; upper and lower sections have drawer arrangements of different numbers and depths to give maximum utility.

HIGHBOY

Hinge The concealed metal joint by which doors and lids are attached; when applied to the outside, hinges are often very decorative; made of brass, bronze, wrought iron.

Hispano Mauresque Style A style reflecting the influence of Moorish craftsmen on the design of southern Spain from about 1300–1600: highly colored glazes on faïence tableware,

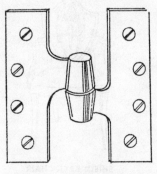

HINGE

wrought-iron accessories and lighting fixtures, tiles, fringed rugs with geometric motifs that are characteristic of North African weaves.

Hitchcock, Lambert (1795–1852) A Connecticut chairmaker; many of his designs were influenced by Sheraton; notably, the black-painted chair with rush seat and stenciled pattern along the back band.

Hobnail Glass A type of milk glass molded into decorative ware; the outer surface is studded with an allover pattern of small domed bumps; it takes its name from a particular kind of nail with a domed head.

HOBNAIL GLASS

Hollow Ware Any metal or ceramic object formed to hold liquids, in contrast to flatware.

Hollywood Bed A pair of twin-size mattresses and box-springs placed on four or six legs; or within a bed frame; may be used with or without a headboard.

Homespun All wool or a blend of wool and other fibers; it has a loose, supple weave, spongy feel, and sometimes tweedy look.

Hooked Rugs Handmade rugs; lengths of yarn are pulled through a heavy canvas-mesh backing, and knotted in back; the top may be left looped or cut to whatever length of pile is required; patterns range from traditional Early American and Provincial primitives to bold contemporary themes; popular as a "do-it-yourself" project.

Horsehair A slick, harsh upholstery fabric tightly woven from mane and tail hairs; although generally a plain weave dyed black, it also has been made in colored stripes and small patterns; first introduced in the late eighteenth century, it has always been associated with the Victorian period.

Host, Hostess Chairs The armchairs matching a set of dining-room side chairs; used at head and foot of table.

Houndstooth Check An old, and almost eternal, small geometric pattern, it is used for either woven or printed fabrics of all kinds; the check is placed diagonally and its four projecting "teeth" interlock; monotone color effects.

HOUNDSTOOTH CHECK

Hue The designation of a pure color such as the three primaries—red, blue, yellow.

Hunt, Peter, Decoration A twentieth-century craftsman identified with a naive, peasantlike, Pennsylvania Dutch type of painted decoration; he developed a trend toward simplifying outmoded and tasteless furniture such as the radio cabinets of the 1920s and turning them into colorful and practical storage units.

Hunt Table A crescent-shaped table high enough for people to stand around and serve themselves a buffet breakfast, which it was designed to hold; in a smaller version it is a popular coffee-table style.

HUNT TABLE

91

Hurricane Lamp A vase-shaped clear glass, globe-type of shade that fits into a candlestick base to protect the flame from wind; lamp may be electrified for use with flame-shaped bulb; the globe may be etched and further embellished with *bobèche* and crystal drops.

Hutch A two-part dining-room case piece: the top is a separate, removable unit with wood-backed shelves for display of china; base is a two-door cabinet raised on legs.

HURRICANE LAMPS

HUTCH

I

Icon A religious painting to be worshiped at home or in the Greek Orthodox and Russian churches; usually it is small, square or rectangular, painted on wood and decorated with *repoussé* silver, gold, precious and semi-precious stones. Greek for image.

Imari Porcelain Porcelain originating in Japan and made solely for export; the design source of many past and present-day china patterns; motifs taken from the elaborate silk brocades woven for the imperial family's kimonos; Imari ware is characteristically red-orange, deep blue, and metallic gold on a white ground; examples are to be found in Derby, Worcester, Spode, and Minton wares in current production as well as among antique collections.

Incandescent Light Standard light bulbs in which a special filament is sealed; incandescent light generates heat while offering brilliance; clear glass bulbs allow maximum light, frosted

IMARI PORCELAIN

bulbs cut down glare, tinted ones suggest cool (blue) or warm (rose) environment.

India Print A lightweight cotton fabric with flowing Indian designs printed on a soft beige or natural-color ground; ready-cut lengths can be used as bedspread throws, made into curtains, etc.; not washable since dyes are not fast color.

Indian Rug Very dense wool pile, sculptured motifs; many derived from ancient Persian and Indian designs, also contemporary geometrics; all have wool fringe edges; colors are subtle and pale.

Inlay Decoration made of small pieces of ivory, mother-of-pearl, contrasting colors and grain of woods, etc. that are inserted into another surface; patterns are intricate and elaborate. (*See* Marquetry.)

Intaglio Semiprecious stones, rock crystal, marble, and other minerals are carved out to picture portrait heads, miniature scenes, etc.; small versions were used with sealing wax as personal seals.

Interior Designer One who is professionally trained to create, plan, supervise, and fulfill the necessary steps in decorating a house or public building; usually members of either the American Institute of Interior Designers (A.I.D.) or of the National Society of Interior Designers (N.S.I.D.), to which they are admitted if they qualify by experience and education; the term "designer" is better suited to the profession than "decorator" since the latter could just as well refer to a house painter, as it does in England.

Iridescent Glass Rainbow colors on clear glass; accomplished by the addition of silver or bismuth to the molten glass.

Ironstone Dense, opaque white material tough enough for hotel dinnerware, florists' urns, and all heavy-duty household ware; in use since the 1880s.

J K

Staffordshire horse, English, eighteenth
century. The Metropolitan Museum of
Art. Bequest of George Blumenthal, 1941.

Meissen candelabrum, German,
eighteenth century. The Metropolitan
Museum of Art. Gift of Ann Payne
Blumenthal, 1943.

Mahogany pole screen with
English eighteenth-
century embroidery. The
Metropolitan Museum of Art.
Exchange, 1949, with
David David.

Commode with marquetry of various woods, Louis XVI.
The Metropolitan Museum of Art. Bequest of
Collis P. Huntington, 1926.

Walnut cabinet with marquetry,
English, late seventeenth
century. The Metropolitan
Museum of Art. Rogers Fund,
1931.

Walnut armchair, English,
seventeenth century. The
Metropolitan Museum of Art.
Fletcher Fund, 1923.

Wing chair, mahogany,
upholstered in printed cotton,
American, eighteenth century.
The Metropolitan Museum of
Art. Gift of Mr. and Mrs.
William A. Moore, 1923.

Side chair, painted in imitation
of Chinese lacquer, English,
eighteenth century. The
Metropolitan Museum of Art.
Gift of Louis J. Boury, 1937.

Desk chair, French, early
nineteenth century. The
Metropolitan Museum of Art.
Gift of Captain and Mrs.
W. G. Fitch, 1910, in memory
of Clyde Hill.

Tea cart. Benchcraft, by Drexel.

Semainier. Benchcraft, by Drexel.

Nest of tables. Benchcraft, by Drexel.

Beechwood day bed, Louis XV. The Metropolitan Museum of Art.
Rogers Fund, 1922.

Ebony desk with brass and tortoise-shell inlay, Louis XIV.
The Metropolitan Museum of Art. Bequest of Ogden Mills, 1937.

Tuxedo sofa. Heritage.

Tambour roll-top desk. Et Cetera Collection, by Drexel.

Mahogany dressing table with ormolu mounts, Bourbon restoration. The Metropolitan Museum of Art. Gift of Mrs. Frederick S. Lee, 1922.

Oak Connecticut chest, American, late seventeenth century. The Metropolitan Museum of Art. Gift of Mrs. Russell Sage, 1909.

Figured silk, Louis XVI.
The Metropolitan Museum of Art.
Rogers Fund, 1940.

Wedgwood chocolate set, English,
eighteenth century. The Metropolitan
Museum of Art. Gift of
Ferdinand Hermann, 1912.

Aubusson rug. Courtesy A. Beshar & Co., Inc.

Chinese rug. Courtesy A. Beshar & Co., Inc.

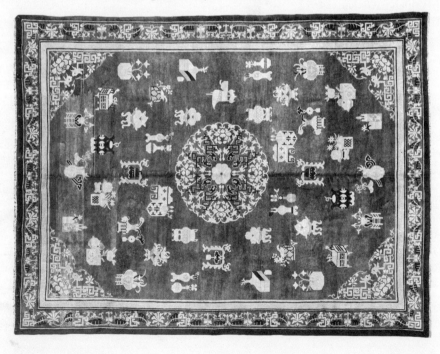

J

Jacobean **(England,** **1600–49)**
The period spanning the reigns of James
I and Charles I of England; architect
Inigo Jones initiated the first revival of
classic styles of antiquity; a continuing
preponderance of massive Italian-style
case furniture; innovations of the period include hinged construction; carved
oak and walnut; crewel embroideries
used decoratively; a trend toward leaf
and bouquet patterns; the dining table
with a set of related chairs, iron and
leather for trimming.

Jacquard Weave Damasks, brocades,
tapestries, "heirloon"-type bedspreads,
table linens, etc. woven on a loom invented by Joseph Jacquard in 1801.
Each warp thread can be controlled individually, resulting in a broad range
of intricate patterns.

Japanned Finish A black (although
other colors may be used) lacquer or
enamel finish developed in an attempt
to duplicate Oriental lacquers; a long-
lasting glossy finish which is built up in

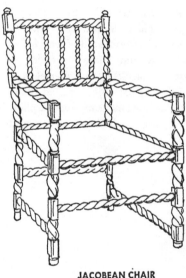

JACOBEAN CHAIR

layers to give a bas-relief, sculptural effect.

Jardinière An ornamental tub or
stand for large plants, indoors or out;
the French word for garden is *jardin*.

97

JARDINIÈRE

Jaspé A fabric woven with a streaky, irregularly striped effect; used for upholstery and slipcovers; the result of varying the colors of the warp yarns.

Jasper Wedgwood's fine stoneware was first made in heavenly blue with white relief carvings; this was followed by other ground colors (lavender, celadon green, black); the material is used primarily for art objects rather than for strictly utilitarian items—vases, plaques, snuff boxes, medallions, and countless other interpretations including men's cuff links.

Julep Cup A drinking vessel shaped like a tall cylindrical glass rather than a cup; made of silver, pewter, stainless steel; for the traditional way of serving mint juleps, other iced beverages; designed in Kentucky about 1795.

JULEP CUP

98

K

Kakemono A Japanese painting on silk or parchment, as a scroll, it may be rolled up like a shade when not on display; unframed even when kept fully opened and hung on a wall.

Kapok A fiber produced from the Malaysian silk-cotton tree; used for filling sofa and bed pillows; although it lacks resilience and can become lumpy, it is widely used for inexpensive merchandise.

Kashan Rug Called the "heavenly" rug; background colors are deep blue or red, sometimes beige; motifs are usually foliage; velvety surface with as many as fifty thousand knots to the foot; very strong and long wearing; made in Iran.

Kidney Shapes Introduced by Sheraton and used by other cabinetmakers of the time; a desk or occasional table with an oval shape scooped out of the center front so that a chair can fit more closely.

KIDNEY-SHAPE TABLE

Kirman Rug Pastel tones, open field with medallion and allover motifs; thick luxurious pile, finely knotted; great durability; made in Iran.

Kitsch Everything that is in poor taste; the misuse of great art works on inappropriate subjects (Da Vinci's "Last Supper" reproduced on an ash tray, for example); also whatever is cheaply vulgar; German for trashy.

99

Klismos An ancient Greek chair which inspired a similar style favored by Directoire and Regency furniture makers; it has a curving back which may have a stenciled decoration or be made of plain wood (less common), or in present-day versions, it may be upholstered; all variations have characteristic splayed front legs; Greek word meaning reclining chair.

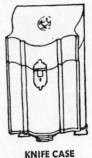

KNIFE CASE

KLISMOS

Knife Rest In the days of multicourse meals, knives and forks were not changed with each new dish; between courses, flat silver was placed on a little glass rest until needed again; these bars, looking like miniature dumbbells made of cut glass or of painted china to match dinnerware patterns, were standard table equipment from about 1850–1900; today they are once again in use, revived for benefit of maidless households; simple modern ceramic rests come from Japan, and there is a vogue for late-antique, fancy cut-glass collectors' items.

Kneehole Desk Any desk with an open area in the center to accommodate the knees; has a pair of drawered pedestals.

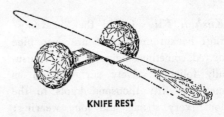

KNIFE REST

Knife Case, or Box An inlaid wood box with sloping front and hinged lift-up top; it was also designed in an urn shape; in either instance, it has been used traditionally to hold cutlery and act as a decorative accessory on sideboard or serving table.

Knockdown Furniture Furniture items that are sold unassembled; the purchaser puts them together and thereby saves on the cost; abbreviated to "KD."

100

LM

L

Lacquer A resinous substance used as a finish on wood or metal; available in black, white, and colors; originally, a natural product made from the sap of trees, it is now manufactured chemically; lacquer is applied in several coats to build up a smooth hard finish; it may also be inlaid in patterns; invented in ancient China, it was a perfected art form there and in Japan by the seventeenth century; typical designs still reflect an Oriental approach to the subjects (landscapes, tiny figures crossing tiny bridges, pagodas, lotus blossoms); overpainting and basic shapes are beginning to show contemporary, modern interpretations.

Ladder-back A chair back having a series of horizontal rails—straight, pierced, or turned; used in one form or another from the seventeenth century up through present-day Chiavari and Scandinavian styles. (*See* Federal American Period.)

Lady Chair A mid-Victorian button-tufted chair with very low, small arms designed to accommodate a hoop skirt; carved wood frame; the style has been simplified into today's slipper or boudoir chair.

LADY CHAIR

Lalique Glass Decorative glass by René Lalique, a leading French designer and craftsman of Art Nouveau and Art Deco periods, also an exponent of Art Moderne; his subjects in glass—vases, perfume bottles, lamp bases, sculptured birds and animals—are readily recognized by their bluish-milky color and smooth uncomplicated surface.

Lambrequin A short overdrapery especially popular in late Victorian times; used for trimming a mantelpiece or to top window draperies.

Lamination A process by which layers of different materials are sealed together; for example, a layer of rigid plastic sheeting may be laminated to wood for extra strength or to create a surface impervious to damage, or an upholstery fabric may be laminated to foam padding to combine the luxury and hand of woven fabric with the suppleness of foam rubber, or a piece of linen may be sealed between two layers of clear plastic to fashion wipe-clean table mats.

Late Antiques Furniture and accessories which fall short of the one hundred year age requirement for antiques, yet have a characteristic style and are being collected by connoisseurs and dealers; e.g., Art Nouveau, 1890s; Art Moderne, 1920s, etc.

Lavabo A two-sectioned washbasin made of ceramic or carved wood; its top section held water; the lower part was a hand basin; both were fastened to a wall; today, the lavabo has become a decorative accessory used as a flower holder or planter.

LAVABO

Lawson Sofa Completely upholstered piece; square back and arms; loose seat cushions and sometimes loose back cushions as well; the Lawson sofa straddles periods—it fits into either traditional or contemporary settings.

Lazy Susan A large circular tray set on a ball-bearing base; made of wood or silver; the top circle revolves and brings foods and condiments within reach of all at the dining table without having to be lifted and passed around; a nineteenth-century innovation.

Lavabo A two-sectioned washbasin to describe table or accessory glassware; generally, it is glass to which soda and lime have been added. (*See* Crystal.)

Leather Upholstery Genuine cowhide is considered ideal for upholstery purposes, and top grain is the finest quality; hides are split into several layers—the topmost one, shorn of its hairs, is the most desirable for appearance and durability. Genuine leather will always be a more expensive upholstery material than even the most extravagant fabric since great skill in handling the skins is of paramount importance; it takes longer, therefore, to upholster with leather than with fabric—the more time expended, the higher the cost.

Library Steps Movable steps with a handrail on one side; upright or spiral in design; used since the eighteenth century as a means of reaching topmost bookshelves in high-ceilinged rooms; some present-day models are used as whatnots or even as lamp tables.

LIBRARY STEPS

Library Table A long, flat-topped table with legs connected by a stretcher; a drawer in the apron; in murky oak or walnut, it has long been virtually the hallmark of a doctor's waiting room.

Lighting *Direct* light focuses light in one direction; *indirect* light, directed upward, is reflected from the ceiling and diffused, providing softer, allover illumination.

Limed Oak Oak pickled with a coating of lime; a whitish residue remains inside the grain of the wood, giving a veined appearance; popular finish for modern furniture of the 1930s and early 1940s.

Limoges Fine French porcelain made since the eighteenth century; usually border-trimmed or with a center medallion, but currently, plain shapes with contemporary lines are being manufactured as well as the traditional styles.

Lincoln Rocker An upholstered rocking chair with gracefully curved, exposed wood frame; very low seat and very tall back; padded armrests; over all, an unusually simple treatment for a Civil War period design.

Linen The oldest known fabric; made of flax, it is often combined with other fibers today; or may be made of 100 per cent rayon (butcher linen); linen is also crewel-embroidered for use as a drapery and upholstery fabric; in all cases, linen is a plain flat weave in a variety of weights, widths, and colors.

Linenfold Carving Vertical carving made to resemble folded linen or parchment scrolls; a Gothic treatment used extensively on chests, chair backs, and wall paneling. (*Illustration page 106.*)

105

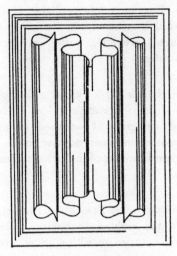

LINENFOLD CARVING

Lion's Head, or Mask A carved lion's head used with the paw foot on a cabriole chair leg; mid-eighteenth-century design revived during the English Regency period.

Loop Pile Pile that is left uncut so that the loops give it textural depth; mainly used for carpeting and upholstery fabrics.

Louis XIV (France, 1643–1715), Louis Quatorze The "Sun King," whose reign saw the realization and completion of the vast palace at Versailles; he encouraged the new splendor that accompanied the structure; his court was fully appreciative of the elaborate, luxurious, self-indulgent mode of life and quickly approved the new designs and decorations; innovations were: inlays, complex veneers, tortoise-shell trim, silk damask and velvet; tall-backed imposing armchairs that looked almost like "everyday" thrones; tapestries of all conceivable designs—from the utilitarian needlepoint furniture coverings to huge wall hangings; many trends were established by the premier *ébéniste* (cabinetmaker) André Boulle, and his marquetry technique subsequently came to be known as Boulle, or Buhl, work; the royal favorites also began to influence the manners and modes as well as the decor of the period.

Louis XV (France, 1723–74), Louis Quinze The Golden Age of French design and decoration; flowering under the refining influence and confident hand of the royal favorite, Madame de Pompadour; her skilled leadership inspired grace, elegance, comfort in every aspect of home (or palace) fashion; soft pastel colors, delicate silk and fine cotton fabrics; sinuous, feminine curves, contoured furniture—even the most rustic; *chinoiserie* accents offered contrast; artistically wrought hardware, rare woods—these are just a few characteristic contributions of this decoratively lush period.

Louis XVI (France, 1774–93), Louis Seize During this period of excesses—whether the extravagances of royalty or that of revolution and radicalism—a seemingly paradoxical trend toward simplicity began to emerge; straighter lines seemed to give furniture a less frivolous appearance than the prevalent curves; fluted legs with applied rosette trim; more dependence upon the classical motifs of antiquity; newly introduced were the all-glass vitrine for displaying collections of objets d'art; restrained applications of festoons, swan and leaf motifs; striped and plain satin upholstery; special pieces of furniture such as the ubiquitous *poudreuse* with its wig-powder and make-up compartments.

LOUIS XIV PERIOD

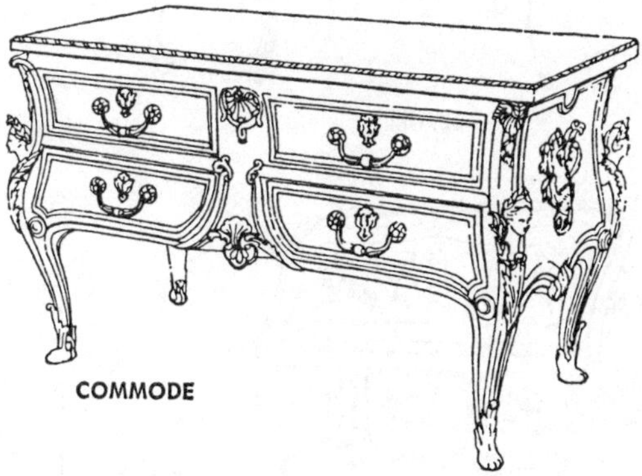

ARMCHAIR

COMMODE

ARMOIRE

LOUIS XV PERIOD

BERGÈRE

SMALL SETTEE

SMALL SLANT-FRONT DESK

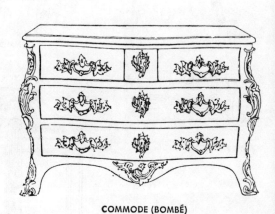

COMMODE (BOMBÉ)

TOILETTE TABLE

LOUIS XVI PERIOD

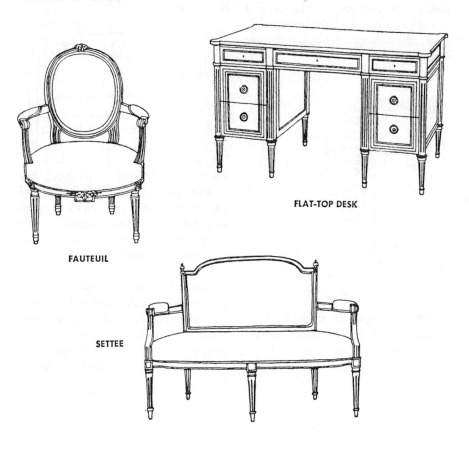

FLAT-TOP DESK

FAUTEUIL

SETTEE

Louvers Shutters made of movable wooden slats that may be raised and lowered to let air and light in; the slats are usually stationary when the shutters are used as doors.

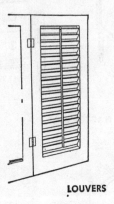

LOUVERS

Love Seat Originally, a double chair; introduced during the Queen Anne period; today, any small sofa—upholstered or with exposed wood frame, with cane or rush seat—wide enough to seat two people.

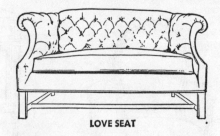

LOVE SEAT

Lunette A favored design motif, it is a half-moon carving used on furniture of various period styles (notably in painted and inlaid versions by the Adam brothers); in architectural use, it is frequently called a fanlight.

Luster A metallic glaze—silver, copper, gold—on china and pottery; may be either the background color with a white pattern showing through or the reverse, with a metallic pattern on a matte-finished white or tinted ground.

M

Macramé The ancient Near Eastern art of knotting tough cord to create fringe or braid; a host of decorative applications: pillow tops, table mats, edging for accent rugs and bedspreads, etc.

Madeira Embroidery Very elaborate cutwork held together by finely overcast connecting bars; exquisitely handmade on the island of Madeira; fabrics are sheer linen and organdy for use as table and luxury bed linens.

MACRAMÉ

MADEIRA EMBROIDERY

Magnolia A wood of pale yellow color; fine grained with a slight marking; a hard and heavy wood for all exposed sections and face veneers.

Mahogany A wood with soft pink to warm reddish tones; may be bleached or kept its natural color, or stained in a range of red to almost black (Cordovan) finishes; texture has tiny pores that look like strawberry seeds; mottles, swirls, figured crotches make mahogany versatile and important as a cabinet wood; choicest varieties come from Central America and Africa; all types of case furniture; veneers, all exposed parts; both period and contemporary styles.

Maple A wood in cream to reddish-brown tones; close grained, dense, tough and does not split; smooth, slick surface with many diverse markings (bird's eye, blister, curly, fiddleback patterns); "hard rock" variety is firmest and of the best quality; all period and contemporary furniture; for any product that requires a versatile, adaptable wood.

Marble A beautifully marked, dense mineral stone whose mottling and veining are never identical in any two slabs; it can be given a high luster and polish or kept slightly roughened; color and patterns vary according to the region— since marble is quarried in almost every country on all continents, its versatility as an architectural material has inspired designers since antiquity; more than three hundred types are in current production and the black, brown, green, ivory, gray, pink, white, rose tones are equally compatible with period and contemporary furnishings.

Mark The identification of a product's origin, its factory or its designer/craftsman; incised on the base of an item or stamped beneath the glaze on ceramics.

Marquetry Variously shaped colored bits of wood are applied in formal patterns to the surface of wood furniture; in appearance, marquetry is much like inlay, but differs in that the shapes are glued to the surface and not inset.

Marquisette Sheer, open-mesh fabric made of synthetic or natural fibers; used for glass curtains in traditional and modern-style rooms.

Martha Washington Sewing Table The name is generally given to a wooden sewing table made with a hinged top above an oval, tublike construction; outside may be fluted or otherwise carved.

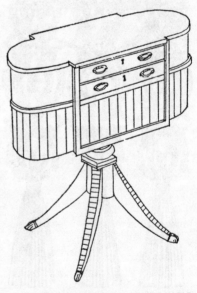

MARTHA WASHINGTON SEWING TABLE

112

Matelassé An upholstery fabric with pattern areas that are slightly puffed and somewhat resemble quilting; the background is plain and tightly woven; of all fibers and mixtures; French word for mattress is *matelas*.

Meissen China Porcelain ware made by one of the earliest production factories in Europe (founded in 1710); best known, perhaps, for its famed "blue onion" pattern on dinnerware and art objects; in the nineteenth century the ware came to be known as Dresden china, after the site of the factory.

Mercury Glass In imitation of silver, it is used primarily for lamp bases and decorative accessories; two layers of clear glass enclose one of silver nitrate and produce the effect of genuine metal; an old technique presently revived, it is used mainly for lamps in plain, round or vaselike shapes topped off with pleated paper or crisp fabric shades.

Milk Glass Opaque white glass with a bluish tinge; made to resemble china rather than glass; for ornamental accessories as well as utilitarian ones, such as covered casseroles, compotes, drinking glasses, candy dishes.

Millefiore Glass Literally, "thousand flowers" in Italian; patterns are blown in innumerable forms—colorful spirals, lozenges, small geometrics, "hard candies"—and are embedded into clear glass spheres for paperweights, doorknobs, drawer pulls, etc.; very popular in Victorian times.

Ming Period (*China, 1386–1644*) One of the best-known, most frequently cited among the antique, Chinese period styles; fine porcelains of this dynasty are characterized by painted decorations rather than solid-color glazes; in addition to delicate blue and white, a strong sulphur yellow color was introduced; this later became the fashion color for fabrics and carpets, continuing its vogue into the English Regency period; enamel colors were also an innovation—used on bisque china without the customary intervening glaze, the effects were texturally brillant and exciting.

Mission-style Furniture A Spanish colonial style common to southwestern United States bordering on Mexico; its simplicity and durability influenced designs of the early twentieth-century; in fact, it was a functional, rectangular forerunner of modern styles.

Miter A method of joining corners; any two pieces of wood, metal, or fabric cut at an oblique angle so that they can be fitted together at right angles.

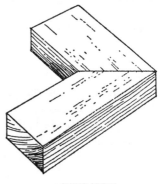

MITER JOINT

113

Mobile A type of abstract sculpture designed to be hung from the ceiling or from a post; the variously shaped elements, suspended from counterbalanced wires, move in the breeze; Alexander Calder, twentieth-century American sculptor, is identified with the art form; it is reminiscent in a way of the old Chinese wind chimes that tinkled in the air currents.

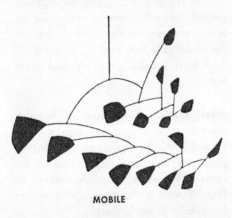

MOBILE

Modern vs. Modernistic Simultaneous with clean-cut, functional modern furnishings emerging from workshops after the First World War, a parallel trend was appearing on the decorative horizon. Opulent, exaggerated movieland castles, proliferating skyscrapers, setback construction, the birth of new plastic materials and finishes were having their influence on the design output of the 1920s and early '30s. "Skyscraper" furniture with setback, step-up construction; busy veneers; oxidized mirrors that gave an eerie blueness to table tops, dressing tables, walls; overscaled, overbleached case furniture, overstuffed and tufted upholstered pieces further embellished with shiny chrome

steel have come to symbolize the modernistic; modernistic is *kitsch* whereas modern is the way of living in one's own times within a surrounding environment that fulfills the requirements of function.

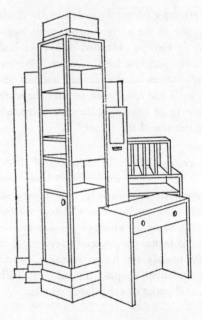

SKYSCRAPER FURNITURE

Modular Furniture Units of sectional furniture that may be stacked vertically one atop the other, or placed side-by-side in horizontal arrangements; all elements within a style group are of the same height and width so that complete interchange is possible; for example, a chest of drawers meshes with a desk; bookshelves can be aligned with any other unit, and so on. (A module is a unit of measure selected as a basis for standardizing sizes of various components.)

114

MODULAR FURNITURE

Mohair An upholstery fabric with a deep cut pile; now made of a variety of fibers although it was originally woven from the wool of a breed of mountain goat.

Moiré Rippled wavy pattern on a finely corded weave; the pattern is created by pressing the fabric between cylinders engraved with the ripple design; the technique originated during the eighteenth-century, and moiré has been a favorite all-purpose decorative fabric ever since; various fibers and blends.

Molding Strips of wood, metal, or other materials which can be applied as an embellishment to walls, furniture, etc.; mostly simple half-round strips give the desired panel effect. (*See* also Egg and Dart, Bolection.)

Monk's Cloth A cotton fabric similar to burlap but finer and smoother, more even in its weave; many colors and width ranges.

Monochromatic Color Scheme A decorative scheme in which one color is used throughout; various tones of the color are included, and black and white (not considered colors) may be added as accents.

Monteith Bowl The grandfather of all punch bowls; its top rim is shaped in such a way that punch cups can be hooked on and suspended into the bowl; the cups could thus be chilled in the ice-cooled punch.

MONTEITH BOWL

Moroccan-style Rug Geometric patterns dominate; straight lines in sharp color contrasts—black, rust, brown—to usually off-white background; pile is very thick, hand-knotted, fringe-edged.

Morris, William (England, 1834–96) An English trend-setting designer, artist, poet, author; he reawakened a latent interest and appreciation of hand crafts; designed the Morris chair—an easy chair with wood frame, upholstered seat, tiltable back; the style continued well into the twentieth-century and is still being manufactured in updated versions; Morris also designed many wallpapers and carpets, drapery and upholstery fabrics with distinctive Gothic and pre-Renaissance pattern derivation.

MORRIS CHAIR

Mortise and Tenon A method of joining wood parts; a rectangular slot (mortise) is cut into a section, and a corresponding projection (tenon) is cut to fit exactly into the mortise.

Mosaic A surface decoration in which small chips of ceramic tile, marble, or stone are set into mortar; the outstanding floor and wall treatment of antiquity, with patterns as literal, complex, and diverse as those found in wall tapestries or painted frescoes; at present, mosaics are being used to lend permanent color to residential and office building lobbies; in a less significant manner, mosaics are seen as table tops, trays, on outdoor furniture, and as a welter of handicraft, do-it-yourself projects.

Moss Fringe A thick short fringe used as trimming to edge the seams of upholstery and slipcovers.

Mother-of-pearl The iridescent, pearly lining of oyster and scallop shell, pieces of which make decorative inlays on table tops, drawer fronts, and various kinds of decorative accessories; in Victorian times, mother-of-pearl was a pop-ular material to use on black papier-mâché boxes, desk sets, etc.

Multifilament Yarns made with several fine strands or filaments twisted together into a single thickness; generally synthetic fibers.

Muntin Construction Wood latticework in which slots allow for the insertion of individual panes of glass; used on upper sections of breakfront cabinets, bookcases.

Mural A wall decoration which may be a painting, mosaic, tapestry, fresco, wallpaper panel, or photographic enlargement.

Muslin A plain weave cotton fabric; can be fine or coarse; often used in an unbleached state; also, sheeting; the phrase "in the muslin" commonly used to describe upholstered furniture before the final outer covering has been selected; the cost then depends upon the quality of the chosen fabric.

Mustache Cup China or earthenware drinking cup of the 1880s and '90s; it had a shieldlike device to protect luxuriant mustaches from beverages; now being revived because of the reappearance of the mustache as a masculine fashion.

Myrtle A wood of light gray-brown color with medium-coarse grain; distinctive dot-and-dash pattern marking; for surfaces and veneers.

NO

N

Needlepoint Tapestry-stitch embroidery worked in wool or floss on canvas or coarse linen and used for pillow covers, rugs, chair seats, wall hangings, pictures; may be no more complex than filling in the background stitches of an already-completed pattern, or the entire subject and background may be worked by the craftsman; a popular form of "lap work."

Neoclassic Decorative style associated with the late eighteenth-century-revival of ancient classical motifs; the Adam brothers were the chief exponents of the style in England.

Nest of Tables Three or four tables of graduated size made to nest within each other; assembled this way, they take the space of only a single table.

Niello The application of black metallic alloy to engraved silver; in this way, the engraved pattern is intensified and stands out in apparent bas-relief from the background.

Ninon Lightweight, finely woven, sheer fabric of various fibers and blends; excellent draping qualities make it favored material for window curtains.

Numdah Rug Small Indian rug of non-woven and feltlike material; hand embroidered with native East Indian motifs which are generally stylized floral; pastel colors; are best used in rooms where the traffic is light.

Nymphenburg Porcelain Fine porcelain made in an important German factory based near Munich; it has been famous since the eighteenth century for sculptured figure groups in rococo style; brilliant blue-white glazes.

119

O

Oak A wood of pale yellow to gray-brown; white and red oak are the major varieties; coarse-grained with obvious growth rings; firm and hard but has a tendency to splinter unless carefully manipulated; golden-oak finish is typical of school desks, old-fashioned office furniture, but the wood takes well to all stains; for all types of indoor and outdoor furniture; period and contemporary, rustic styles.

Obelisk Four-sided, tapering, miniature column made of marble, crystal, ormolu, and now even plastic; used singly as a decorative accessory or as the base of a clock, candelabrum, lamp; it represents a memento of Napoleon's Egyptian campaigns since the form was inspired by the huge stone obelisks that marked the North African landscape.

Objets d'Art Objects valued for their intrinsic beauty and exceptional workmanship. A monumental marble sculpture and a miniature china figurine may or may not survive the same criteria—

OBELISK

the figurine could easily outrank the mammoth figure in artistic purpose; measurement and cost do not make an objet d'art (French for work of art); a Meissen porcelain thimble ¾-inch high will have greater worth than a dubious 30×40-foot oil painting of kittens in a basket.

Occasional Furniture Small items of furniture such as lamp and coffee tables,

121

magazine racks, serving carts, portable bars, etc.; any similar items that are used as accent pieces.

Oil Finish Oil is rubbed into wood surfaces to produce a soft glow as opposed to a stain, varnish, or lacquer finish. Preferable to a too-glossy sheen on contemporary teak and walnut furniture.

Ombré A shaded effect created by graduated tints of one color; an ombré stripe on wallpaper or fabric repeats these shadings across the width of the material.

Op Art Optical illusion, movement, and rhythm stemming from the juxtaposition of patterns and colors; lines wave, radiate, wiggle; engage the eye with motion rather than narrative content.

Open Stock China, glass, or flat silver which may be bought by the individual piece at any time as needed; available until the manufacturer decides to make the pattern "inactive."

Organdy Plain weave in the finest, sheerest cotton, silk (called organza), or nylon; it has a rather crisp hand, lends itself to ruffled spreads and curtains; frequently allover Schiffli-embroidered.

Oriental Rug Designation for handwoven or hand-knotted rugs native to the Middle and Far East; the patterns may be geometric or stylized floral with center motifs, borders; Turkish, Persian (Iranian), Indian, Chinese designs have their own individual and unmistakable characteristics; all genuine oriental rugs are made of wool, wool mixed with silk, or all-silk yarn.

Ormolu Gilded bronze used mostly for lamp mounts, candelabra, wall sconces; often combined with black for contrast; widely used in France during the Empire period and in England during the Regency.

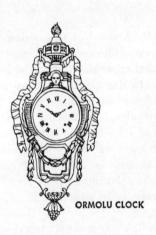

ORMOLU CLOCK

Ottoman A boxlike, armless, cushioned seat upholstered in any number of adaptable materials from cut velvet to wet-look vinyl; it may match an upholstered lounge chair and be pulled up to it as a foot rest or a dual-purpose chaise longue.

Ox Blood Distinctive, dark, rust-red glaze used on antique Chinese decorative accessories; often referred to as *sang de boeuf*, the French words for the color.

122

P Q

P

Pagoda A many-sided storied tower with graceful upturned corners, hanging bells; a temple or sacred building in India, China, Japan; it was used in miniature scale by Chippendale and other eighteenth-century cabinetmakers during the vogue for *chinoiserie;* this amusing decorative style was frequently the fash-ion for bird cages, hanging shelves, mirror tops, bed canopies; sometimes gilded, sometimes lacquered red or apple green; sometimes made entirely of bamboo or rattan.

Paisley A timeless pattern used on fabric, wallpaper, carpets; originated in Paisley, Scotland, as the fringed wool shawl worn in the mid-1800s; its swirling, abstract leaf shapes are generally multicolored and traceable to ancient Persian designs; contemporary stylists

PAGODA

PAISLEY

favor the effectiveness of paisley motifs printed in monotones like charcoal or black on white for present-day materials.

Palladian Style Introduced by the sixteenth-century Italian architect Palladio, its classic, columned, Roman public-monument style has continued as a dominant influence on building since its inception.

Panne Velvet Cut pile (silk, nylon, rayon) is pressed down in one direction to give a satinlike surface with great sheen.

Paperweight A decorative weighty object for holding down desk papers and pamphlets; often a collector's item made of clear glass in spherical or bun shapes, or in many-faceted cuttings, in bronze, minerals, etc.; countless designs and symbols may be embedded within clear materials: e.g., *millefiore* glass motifs, dried flowers, sea horses, shells, nuts and bolts, coins and medals, etc.; an enduring style is the snowfall weight in which tiny white flecks seem to whirl in miniature blizzard fashion when the weight is lifted and gently shaken.

Papier-mâché An amalgam of materials (wood shavings, paper pulp, glue, flour and water) mixed into a malleable easy-to-mold substance; when dry, it is rigid and long lasting; used for small, occasional furniture, desk accessories, boxes, etc.; a favorite pastime material in past and present times.

Parian Ware Bisque china used instead of marble or stone for small-scale statuary during the Victorian period, in particular; its cool whiteness was a perfect material for the millions of little replicas of the Parthenon, Roman Pantheon, busts of Homer and Shakespeare that rested on whatnots or library bookshelves.

Parquetry Inlaid geometric patterns formulated especially for hardwood flooring; a design technique that began in the seventeenth century and has continued into the present.

Parsons Table An undecorated square or rectangular table in a range of sizes; named for the Parsons School of Design (training ground for many noted interior designers) where it was said to have been conceived as a student-project assignment; leg and apron widths are the same dimension; the table is finished in many brilliant enamel or lacquer colors, a variety of woods, glass, and metal; may be covered in patterned vinyl plastic, or in printed self-stick materials; sizes from 15-inch square to full dining-room table scale.

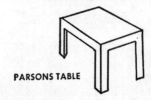

PARSONS TABLE

Partners' Desk Eighteenth- and nineteenth-century business partners often used this impressive oversized desk: it was two-sided, with what seemed to be two desks placed back to back, but it really was a one-piece construction providing two sets of drawers, file space; sometimes with tooled-leather top.

Patera Small ornamental disks with lightly carved designs (such as the rosette); taken from sacrificial cups of antiquity; used in a variety of decorative applications.

PATERA

Patina The natural finish that age and careful polishing bring to a wood surface; copied by manufacturers of high-priced furniture to suggest care, age, constant polishing.

Peacock Chair An all-wicker armchair with a huge fan-shaped, flaring back; a low round seat and flush base; the stock décor in most South Pacific movie settings; very popular during Victorian times when tea planters brought the chairs back to England on their return from Malaysia.

Pecan A wood native to the southern United States; has a warm medium-brown color and a smooth grain; used for occasional furniture in combination with other cabinet woods; for plywood paneling.

Pedestal Table Any table (occasional or of dining size) which has a center post for support; often the post ends in a tripod leg arrangement; a typical Duncan Phyfe treatment. (*See* Regency.)

Pediment A triangular topping to a building; an ancient Greek and Roman architectural feature, it has been copied in wood to top off a bookcase, chest-on-chest, breakfront, etc.; especially typical of Federal American period design. (A broken pediment is illustrated.)

PEDIMENT

Pegboard A man-made material molded into panels and perforated with small holes at regular intervals into which hooks can be inserted; any kind of object from kitchen utensils to framed art works can be hung from these panels.

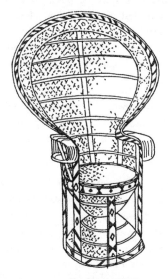

PEACOCK CHAIR

127

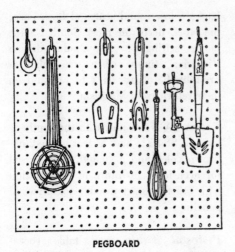

PEGBOARD

Pelmet Overtrim, cornice, or valance that conceals drapery and curtain hardware; it is a term more commonly used in England than in the United States.

Pembroke Table Extremely popular and versatile rectangular, occasional table style; the hinged leaves at the sides may be raised to square off the top and give extra surface space; usually fitted with a small drawer; sometimes has a tooled-leather top.

PEMBROKE TABLE

Pennsylvania Dutch Not Dutch at all in origin, it is a traditional folk-art style of decoration introduced by Swiss and German settlers who came to Lancaster and York counties in Pennsylvania during the seventeenth and eighteenth centuries; they brought along colorful stenciled designs which were applied to chests, occasional pieces, trunks, wardrobes, kitchenware; typical motifs were the tulip, heart, bird (the "distelfink"), and hex signs; pine and walnut woods, and dark painted finishes are characteristic.

Percale Plain weave, lightweight cotton made at least 180 threads to the square inch; the fewer the threads, the coarser the fabric and the rougher the texture; also made of polyester yarns or of combinations of cotton and polyester fibers.

Pewter An alloy of tin and lead or other metal producing a gray material; used for hollow ware and flat serving accessories; it may be polished to a high luster or left matte-finished; less formal and cruder in workmanship than silver or stainless steel, it fits well into provincial and casual modern decorative schemes.

Photomural A giant-sized enlargement made from a sharp negative; mounted first on wallboard, then framed or not, and attached to a wall.

Phyfe, Duncan (New York, 1768–1854) America's most famous traditional furniture name; his workroom and shop were established in New York City; designs were noticeably influenced by French First Empire styles and certain Sheraton details; characteristic of

PITCHER

CHESTS

DUNCAN PHYFE DESIGNS

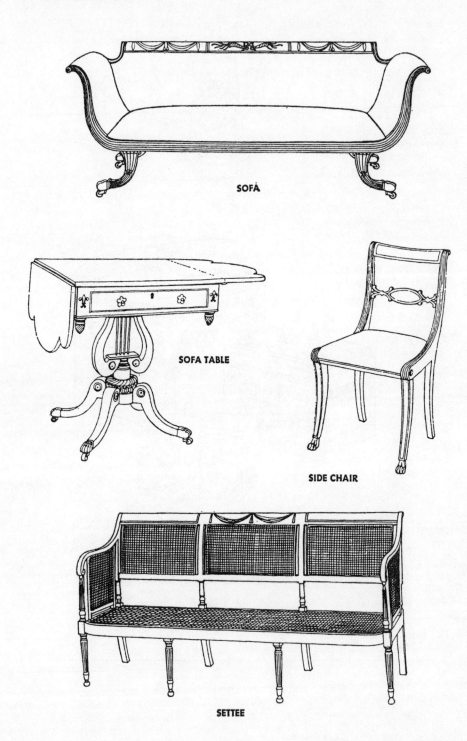

SOFA

SOFA TABLE

SIDE CHAIR

SETTEE

his own style, the lyre form in chair backs and table pedestal; rosewood, a favored wood; as a design category, Phyfe's cabinetwork belongs to the overall Federal period, while in some instances foreshadowing early Victorian trends.

Pickled Finish White paint is rubbed into previously stained and finished woods to create an antique effect; the grain absorbs the white and lends a striped look.

Picture Window A room-wide glass window, originally created to frame a picturesque scene or view.

Piecrust Table Tilt-top, round occasional table with scalloped edge that suggests the fluting around a home-baked pie; mid-eighteenth century, American and English.

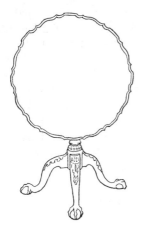

PIECRUST TABLE

Pier Glass A tall, slender, framed mirror designed to fit between a pair of windows, above a fireplace, or into a narrow wall panel.

Pilaster A column or post in low relief attached to building façade or an interior wall; as an applied carving, to trim the front of cabinets and desks.

PILASTER

Pile Fabrics Woven fabrics with cut or uncut loops which stand rather than lie flat; weaves that include velvet, plush, corduroy, bouclé, friezé; in carpeting, height or density of pile determines the quality of rugs and carpets.

Pilgrim, or Puritan, Furniture The name given by antiquarians and interior designers to the earliest, simple wood furniture made in seventeenth-century America.

PILGRIM CHEST

131

Pinch Pleat The heading most frequently chosen to finish a drapery; a cluster of three pleats is tightly stitched together at the base and left open to fan out slightly at the top; depth is generally at least three inches.

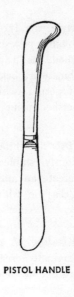

PISTOL HANDLE

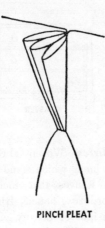

PINCH PLEAT

Pine Pale cream color wood with an even texture; numerous knots left in for decorative purposes; used for framework, kitchen cabinets, unpainted furniture, wall paneling.

Pipkin A tiny copper or brass saucepan with a disproportionately long handle; for heating and serving melted butter; to heat brandy for crêpes suzettes and other *flambé* dishes.

Pistol Handle Many eighteenth-century silver knives were designed with a rounded, incurving handle patterned after the grip of a dueling pistol; when made of painted porcelain, often used for fruit and dessert sets, salad serving pieces.

Place Setting The combination of china or silver pieces that may be required for one person to use at meals. Silver and china are bought more conveniently in five- or six-piece settings than in complete sets of so many dozens of individual items; the five-piece china setting consists of a dinner plate, salad or dessert plate, bread and butter plate, cup, saucer; the standard six-piece flat silver, silver plate, or stainless steel setting consists of a dinner knife, dinner fork, salad or dessert fork, butter knife, tea spoon (a second tea spoon is sometimes substituted for the individual butter knife).

Plaque As a small medallion made of wood, porcelain, or ormolu, it is applied as decoration on furniture; in a large size, it is treated as a picture in a wall arrangement.

132

Plinth The boxlike square base on which a column rests.

Plissé Fabric with an effect similar to seersucker but produced by a chemical process that shrinks certain areas; seersucker is woven to give the crinkled surface. Both versions are used for bedspreads, curtains, blanket covers; cotton, rayon, nylon, polyester fibers; word is French for crumpled, crinkled.

Plywood Several thin sheets or strips of wood are glued together with the grain of one layer going in a right-angle direction from the alternating one; a process used today in all major categories of furniture manufacture for built-in cabinets and shelving.

Point d'Esprit A lace or lacelike fabric in which tiny embroidered dots are scattered over a sheer net, base fabric; a lightweight curtain material that resembles millinery veiling.

Pole Screen An eighteenth-century firescreen designed to keep direct heat away from the face when in front of an open fire; a needlework or brocade panel on a tripod-base pole which could be raised or lowered; Chippendale designed several of these graceful, individual screens.

Pomander Made of a whole dried orange studded with cloves and spices; may also be a pottery or china container filled with sweet-smelling potpourri; both versions are suspended from ribbons and act as room refreshers.

Ponderosa Pine A wood of yellow to red-brown color with smooth texture and profuse knotholes; durable, easy to manipulate; same uses as plain pine.

Pop Art A phenomenon of the 1960s, it dignified everyday subjects—tomato ketchup bottles, soup cans, movie posters, comic strip personalities—and rendered them in faultless, literal, painstaking style.

Poplar Wood that has lightly streaked markings on greenish-tinged yellow and pale brown colorings; straight, even textured; can be stained to resemble mahogany or walnut; used for crossbandings; veneers made from its burls; as framework for medium-price case pieces; piano sounding boards.

Porringer A shallow bowl or cup with one flat, pierced handle at the rim; pewter or silver, it was originally a child's drinking cup, but is now popularly used as a serving accessory or ash tray.

PORRINGER

Porter's Chair Rediscovered recently by trend-making interior designers; a high-backed, semicircular, leather-covered, nail-studded armchair which virtually encloses the sitter and protects him from drafts; introduced as long ago as the sixteenth century for use in chilly hallways and entrances.

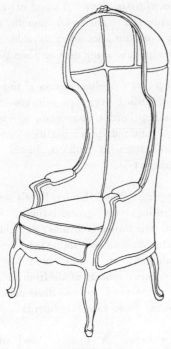

PORTER'S CHAIR

Poster Art A present-day art form whose original purpose was to announce or advertise a variety of local events: exhibitions, fairs, concerts, opera, transportation, etc.; posters are collected for their stylized, colorful, and artistic interpretations of the particular subject; many famed painters have created poster art—Chagall, Dali, Picasso, and, notably, Toulouse-Lautrec.

Pot de Crème Set Six or more fine porcelain miniature tureens with covers and a matching tray; usually decorated in metallic gold, with hand-painted floral motifs, etc.; for serving a gourmet chocolate cream dessert, pudding, custard; *pot de crème,* French for pot of cream.

Potpourri Dried flowers, herbs, and spices are mixed into fragrant formulas to be used as room fresheners and sachets; kept in china jars molded with pierced lids that allow the scent to escape.

Poudreuse Originally, an eighteenth-century French vanity table with a lift-up mirror above a center well; today, the well is used to house cosmetics and not as the wig-powder catchall which was its primary function.

Pouf A large round ottoman usually covered in velvet or satin and deeply tufted; leather and vinyl fabrics have replaced the more delicate materials for today's needs.

Prayer Rugs Very small Oriental rugs that have a central motif representing an altar in a mosque; a devout Moslem kneels on the rug so that his forehead touches the pointed arch in the pattern; these little rugs are collector's items and are more likely to be hung on a wall than stepped upon in foyer or entryway.

Pre-Victorian Period (England, 1820–37) This brief interval heralded the development of furniture making as a factory industry; suites of dining-room and parlor furniture were introduced into general household use, made attainable because of lowered costs

134

due to new machine, assembly-line methods; metal (cast and wrought iron, brass) indicated a coming revival of the Gothic; rosewood, mahogany, and other dense woods were carved and polished to excess; the acquisition of antiques became a new status symbol—these were mainly Elizabethan and Jacobean designs.

Pricket Candleholder A candlestick with a projecting spike rather than a recessed cup for holding the taper; early ones were very ornate and tall enough to balance candles that were often five inches in diameter; these were intended for church use; made of wrought iron, brass, pewter; presently being used as accessories in Spanish-, Moroccan-, Southwestern-styled decorative schemes.

PRICKET
CANDLEHOLDER

Primary Colors The three fundamental colors—red, blue, yellow—which cannot be mixed from one another; all other colors are derived from proportionate mixtures of any two of these three.

Primavera Wood that is creamy-to-

pale yellowish brown with a small pinhole grain that looks like mahogany; it is even called white mahogany, a term disallowed by the U. S. Federal Trade Commission; used for face veneers, applied trims on period-style furniture, and for complete pieces of modern-style case furniture.

Priming Coat The first, underlying coat of paint used to seal surface pores; to cover slight inperfections before final paint is applied.

Prince of Wales Plumes A decorative wood carving patterned after the three ostrich feathers that form the Prince of Wales's crest; a device Hepplewhite frequently adapted for a chair back.

PRINCE OF WALES PLUMES

Printed Fabric and Wallpaper Two processes are used: metal *rollers* which are engraved with the pattern or the *silk screen* method. Roller prints are less expensive since they need no hand oper-

135

ation; a separate engraving is made for each color within the pattern, the fabric or wallpaper go through as many printings as there are colors in the design; it is a rapid, mechanized process used since the eighteenth century. Screen or hand printing is a slower, more painstaking, and costly operation; each color is printed separately through a fabric screen cut expressly for it; paint or dye is forced through the sheer fabric (nylon, silk) and onto the piece goods or paper; the steps are hand-guided although the actual process has also become mechanized. (*See* also Serigraph.)

PRISCILLA CURTAINS

Priscilla Curtains Cape Cod, Early American style of full-length window curtains; ruffled all around, tied back at each side; may use matching ruffled valance; all sheer crisp fabrics, especially organdy; also percale with eyelet embroidery trim.

Pullman Kitchen A present-day urban apartment kitchen arranged in a long narrow area; like the Pullman railroad car from which it takes its name, all the necessary appliances are lined up against one wall, thereby using minimum floor space.

Q

Quartered Oak Oak and other woods first cut into quarters, then sliced across the four sections, producing decorative effects when the raylike markings are rearranged.

Quartetto A nest of four tables. (*See* also Nest of Tables.)

Queen Anne (England, 1702–14) In the style developed during the reign of Queen Anne, decoration came of age—it assumed for the first time in history a planned, preconceived character; the growing refinement of taste, an increasing desire for elegance and gentility soon had their beneficent influence upon the home; Oriental styles appeared everywhere; new additions were the cabriole leg with claw-and-ball foot, small occasional pieces for specific functions; fiddle- and splat-back chairs; more interesting colors and textures brought new flair to the decorative scheme of things; and standards of cabinetmaking were set for all time; this simple but elegant style is one with sur-

prising adaptability to contemporary use when combined with sleek modern furnishings. (*Illustration page 138.*)

Queen's Ware Wedgwood earthenware—both antique and that presently manufactured—has a cream-white body and a raised border; simple fluting or a vine and leaf wreath; although the tradition has been to keep the border white, touches of leaf green or Wedgwood blue are sometimes added.

Quilting A process of making a thick, warm, decorative material; two fabrics with cotton wadding or a polyester fiber-

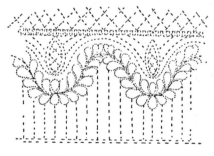

QUILTING PATTERN

fill between; held together by means of straight stitching through all the layers; stitching patterns are usually geometric—diamond, square, overlapping rings; a more sophisticated look is achieved when a printed motif is outlined and the rest of the fabric is left plain; used for upholstery, bedspreads, comforters, closet accessories, etc.

Quimper Pottery A town in Brittany (northern France) noted for its gay peasant pottery; designs are hand-painted and usually feature male and female figures as a center motif, primitive border designs; all are rendered in primary colors.

QUEEN ANNE PERIOD

DESK

HIGHBOY

SIDE CHAIR

TEA TABLE

138

R S

R

Rabbet A strip of wood with drilled holes or grooves that allows another piece of wood to be inserted; this is the customary method of installing pegged bookshelves and other wall-hung units; rabbeted strips are nailed to a wall and the pegged cabinets and shelves are fitted in.

Random Shearing A manner of clipping certain loops on a carpet surface so that a pattern of high/low, cut/uncut pile results.

Reading, or Music, Stand An adjustable sloping easel, sometimes intricately carved, is set on a tripod base; holds a heavy book or sheet music at eye level.

Reclining Chair A mechanized lounge chair on which the back can be

READING STAND

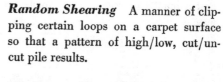

RECLINING CHAIR

lowered, the foot panel raised; can be adjusted to any degree of tilt; allover tufted upholstery, or wood frame and fabric combinations.

Redwood A wood of pale red tone; smooth textured with many burls which lend great surface interest; the oldest living tree, it grows to vast height and enormous girth; widely adaptable to wall paneling, outdoor furniture; decorative veneers are made from the burls.

Reeding Low-relief carved trim for furniture; its convex, vertical lines suggest a bundle of reeds; used chiefly on legs.

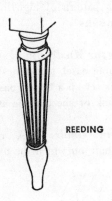

REEDING

Refectory Table A long dining table with heavy pedestals at each end, elaborately carved; originated in monasteries and schools where community dining was the practice.

Régence Period (France, 1715–23) The Régence years came between the death of Louis XIV and the accession of Louis XV to the throne of France; less grand, perhaps, than its immediate pred-

ecessor, but not yet as curvaceous as the style to emerge under the devoted guidance of Madame de Pompadour; this brief period saw the further development of case furniture—the chiffonier, commode, *escritoire*—all designed with specific functions to be filled.

Regency Period (England, 1800–20) The years in England when the Prince of Wales acted as prince regent before becoming George IV; influenced markedly at first by the neighboring French First Empire modes, but only until its own lighthearted, sometimes precious, style was launched; the talented leadership of Beau Brummel as the trend maker and an appreciative monarch as sponsor were a forceful influence on design; there was intense interest in *chinoiserie;* in the shapes and decorations of classical Greece and Rome, then under excavation; and even the design elements carried over from the preceding Georgian periods seemed to assume a newly burnished elegance and refinement; the period brought spring construction to give upholstered furniture new-found comfort; the inclusion of a dressing table as a necessity in the total decorative setting became a virtual trade-mark of this clothes-conscious time; bamboo and cane, bronze and brass, Bristol blue and other clear colors in opaline glass are also highlights of the Regency style.

LAMP TABLE

ARMCHAIR

PEDESTAL TABLE

BOOKCASE

Renaissance Period (from 1300 in Italy, from 1400 to 1600 in other European countries) The word is French, meaning rebirth; for this was the time in recorded history that defines the transition between the Middle Ages and modern times; it was the unparalleled era of reawakened desire for learning—in art, architecture, science, the humanities, music, and, far from irrelevant, in home decoration. The Renaissance came to Italy earlier than to

143

other lands because Italy was never really attuned to Gothic attitudes, never found the style compatible to climate or terrain; the wave of learning quickly spread across Europe bringing in its wake revolutionary social changes, religious reformation; the invention of mechanical printing in the mid-fifteenth century made interchange of ideas and information possible and powerful. The three-hundred-year period is divided roughly into three stages of development: early Renaissance, 1320–1450; high or classic Renaissance, 1450–1550; and late Renaissance (into the Baroque) from 1550–1610; for description of style changes within the overall period, refer to definitions under Gothic, Tudor, Elizabethan, Jacobean, Baroque.

Rep A sturdy, multipurpose weave resembling dress-weight ottoman; it has horizontal ribs of one thickness; made of all fibers.

Repoussé The ornate raised pattern produced by hammering a design from the inside or back of an object; used mostly for silver; many copper and brass accessories from the Middle East also feature the technique.

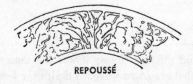
REPOUSSÉ

Reproduction A copy of a fabric, rug, wallpaper, furniture, or any item that was designed in an earlier time.

An exact copy in every detail is usually referred to as an authentic reproduction. If there's too much deviation in a copy, it is generally called an adaptation.

Resist Print An ancient method (there is evidence of its use in biblical times in Egypt) of printing one color on a white or tinted fabric; areas not to be dyed are covered with wax or other pigment-resistant substance; after dyeing, the wax is removed.

Restoration Furniture, china, glass, tapestry, etc. that have been brought back to their original condition through skillful replacing of missing parts or by expert reconstruction; it differs from *repair*, which defines the mending of a broken element without adherence to authenticity of detail or the specialized historical knowledge necessary.

Reveal The space between a window frame and the face of a wall; its depth varies from shallow to wide enough to accommodate a built-in seating unit or storage chest.

Revere Bowl A beautifully proportioned, undecorated all-purpose bowl designed by Paul Revere in 1768 (at that time it was named the Sons of Liberty bowl); it is so chastely classic in con-

REVERE BOWL

tour that it fits into the most modern interior; copies are available in a range of sizes; in solid silver or in silver plate.

Ribbon-back Chair An open armchair with rippling, interlaced wood bowknots and ribbonlike carvings in the back; often a Chippendale design.

RIBBON-BACK CHAIR

Rice-grain Pattern A type of decoration used by contemporary ceramics designers; derived from antique Chinese and Persian porcelain; tiny grain-shaped perforations were cut into the surface of a bowl or vase; which were later filled in with a translucent glaze to give a light-and-shade effect when held to the light.

Rising Sun Resembling an opened fan, this ornament is typically Federal American in feeling; it provides the major trimming on highboys, chests, desks, table legs.

RISING SUN

Rocaille Carved and painted ornamentation simulating rock formations; the basic design element of the rococo styles of early eighteenth-century French and Italian, later German and Austrian modes; French word means rock work.

Rococo Elaborate style of decoration and architecture featuring *rocaille* (*see* above) and *coquille* (the shell) design elements; said to have been inspired by a back-to-nature trend; but nature is rarely as complex in its forms as this decoration applied to walls, ceiling, furniture, accessories, furniture in the early eighteenth century; the fashion endured until a reaction set in and the desire for greater simplicity brought a return of classicism.

Rosette A flat, stylized rose made of wood, bronze, stone, or brass, depending on where it would be applied; on mirrors and picture frames, rosettes are usually placed at the corners; on furniture, at the junction of chair leg and apron.

ROSETTE

Rosewood A wood of purple-brown to almost black color; dense, hard, and heavy with a distinctive vertical grain; when cut, the wood gives off a scent of roses; a favored wood in Victorian times for pianos, sofa and chair frames; in present-day decoration, rosewood is sometimes combined with glass and steel; used for wall paneling and many types of wall-hung cabinets and shelves that co-ordinate with the panels.

Rush Seating Rush, one of the oldest materials known to man, has been used since biblical times; it is tubelike grass that grows in or near water; pliancy makes it easy to weave into mats, baskets, chair backs and seats; rush seating has an affinity to casual, informal furniture styles—French Provincial, Early American, and the currently popular Chiavari chair.

Rya Rug Accent rug made in Scandinavian countries; hand-knotted shaggy weave with alternating short and long pile; abstract contemporary or traditional peasant-type designs in bold colorings; all versions used in informal decorative settings.

S

Saddle Seat A chair seat shaped to resemble a saddle; solid wood with two shallow depressions that flank a center ridge; characteristic of Windsor chairs; it might even be among the earliest experiments at contour seating.

Sailcloth A cotton fabric of canvaslike construction and strength in flat weave; takes readily to prints and bold colors.

Sandalwood An Indian wood, light brown in color with a long-lasting, pungent scent (also used as the base for perfume); soft and pliable, used mainly for folding screens, boxes, small chests, decorative accessories.

Sandwich Glass Glassware on which lacy allover patterns are pressed via molds; a wide variety of motifs and subjects; clear or palely tinted (light yellow-green, for example); originally made by the Boston & Sandwich Glass Company from 1825 to the late 1880s; has been in constant manufacture up to the present; as a classification, it is a collector's item as well as a very widely admired multipurpose ware.

SANDWICH GLASS

Sarouk Rug Floral motifs arranged on deep rose or blue ground; very heavy weight (some $9{\times}12$-feet sizes weigh more than one hundred pounds); designs cover background densely, with framed medallions the dominant feature; made in western Iran.

Sateen Smooth, slick, all-cotton fabric with the same weave as silk satin; is known by several well-advertised names such as Glosheen, polished cotton, etc.

Satinwood A wood of golden color; satinlike grain with natural luster; rib-

147

bon-stripe markings, sweet odor; used for borders and inlays since it combines well with other woods.

Savonarola Chair, see Dante Chair

Sawbuck Table An American innovation, the roughhewn removable top is set on an X-shape base; bench seats are sometimes attached; outdoor, picnic type of rustic furniture.

SAWBUCK TABLE

Scagliola A simulation of real marble made of a mixture of plaster of Paris, glue, cement, with random fragments of marble; used for top surfaces of occasional furniture, console and game tables; an Italian innovation popular in eighteenth-century England and France.

Scandinavian-style Rug Flat-woven, often reversible; or deep shaggy, twisted yarns; all designs are contemporary and colors range from subdued monotones to brilliant combinations of orange, red, pink, turquoise, olive; peasant folk-art patterns and modern allover motifs.

Schiffli Embroidery A machine-made

embroidery with considerable versatility, it is presently used on every type of fashion item from lingerie to bedspreads and curtains; many home-fashion patterns are fruit and flower motifs, trailing vines, border traceries.

Sconce A wall bracket, often branched, designed to hold candles; can be wired for use with electric bulbs.

SCONCES

Scotchgard Finishing process applied to upholstery fabrics to make them soil resistant, able to be cleaned with a wet cloth; a trade-mark name.

Scrimshaw A folk art form; pieces of polished whalebone carved or incised to make small decorative objects; it is said that the craft was a pastime for sailors making long voyages on clipper ships early in the nineteenth century; the term also refers to the extravagant wood carvings which trimmed late Victorian cottage architecture.

148

SCRIMSHAW

Second Empire Period (France, 1852–70), Napoleon III Victorian styles finally took root in France which had seemed reluctant to abandon First Empire fashions; fewer excesses characterize the furniture and furnishings, due probably to the taste and refinement of the Empress Eugénie; one of the items that may be specifically attributed to the Second Empire is the huge velvet-covered and tufted pouf that was often the center of attraction in the decorative scheme; chairs and sofas were smaller scaled than their English and American counterparts; silk taffeta multicolor plaids and rainbow stripes, eyelet-embroidered muslin (*broderie anglaise*), rich blond lace were among the favored fabrics of the period.

Secondary Colors Colors that are made by mixing equal parts of two primary colors—green (blue+yellow), violet (red+blue), orange (red+yellow); tertiary colors—blue-green, yellow-green, blue-violet, red-violet, red-orange, yellow-orange—flank each secondary color on the color wheel; they add a measure of a primary color to a secondary.

See-through Furniture A current descriptive term for occasional furniture made of glass, clear plastic (acrylic, such as Lucite); when placed over an accent rug, a glass coffee table reveals the colorful pattern below; a plastic *étagère*, used as a room divider, does not completely block the view.

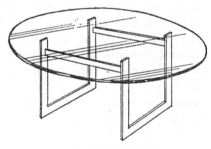

SEE-THROUGH TABLE

Semainier A seven-drawer chest planned to hold the wearing apparel and accessories set aside for each day of the week; a tall, slender piece, made in painted or stained wood finishes; in the various eighteenth-century styles as well as modern versions; *semaine* means week in French.

Serigraph, or Silk Screen A printing process that forces pigment through a series of screens made of sheer fabric (silk or nylon) onto paper and cloth; colors have a slightly raised texture which distinguishes them from other forms of printing; colors are brilliant, opaque and flat; some serigraphs are screened directly to the artist's material to give the effect of original brush painting.

Serpentine The snakelike curve that shapes a cabinet or dresser front (concave-convex-concave); different from a bombé front which is one convex curve.

SETTEE

Service Plate A china plate (contemporary settings also favor tin, pewter, silver) that may match a dinnerware pattern but usually does not; about an inch larger than the standard dinner plate, it is used under the first courses (cocktail, soup, fish) of a formally planned dinner; it is not removed until the main course is brought to the table; its purpose is to have a plate at the place setting at all times during the meal.

Settee A two- or three-seat sofa with open wood frame, back and arms; the seat may be wood, rush, cane, or fabric covered; Early American, Hepplewhite, Sheraton, and simple Shaker designs.

Settle One of the earliest seating units (since Gothic times); the nineteenth-century style has a high back and seat set on a flush base above two drawers; a pair of these all-wood settles was usually placed at either side of a fireplace; the standard-height style is also of all-wood construction, made with a lift-up

hinged seat that doubles as a storage unit.

Sèvres Porcelain Famous French porcelain of superlative quality made in a factory founded in the mid-eighteenth century; appropriated by Louis XV as his private source of table and decorative china; Sèvres blue is a unique blue glaze which has a faint green undertone.

Sgraffito Scratch-decorated pottery was a popular Pennsylvania Dutch craft, and many contemporary Italian, Scandinavian, and American potters have rediscovered the technique; an object is coated with slip (liquid clay), and motifs and borders are incised while the surface is moist; the object may then be glazed or left dull before firing. Italian for scratched.

Shadow Box A wood frame with a deep reveal all around; used for displaying small curios (coins, medals, shells, stones, etc.); it is usually lined with a fabric suited to the collection (deep-hued velvet, ecru or light gray linen, etc.); this type of frame is often used to enhance modern paintings and graphics where a sense of depth is desirable.

Shaker Furniture A clean-lined austere style of furniture, native American in origin, made by a religious sect that flourished in the nineteenth century; from New York State it traveled as far west as Indiana; designs, mainly for the Shakers' own use, were noted for their functionalism and utter simplicity.

SHAKER CHAIR

Sham Decorative cover of a bed pillow; although a separate unit, it usually matches the bedspread.

Shaving, or Box, Mirror A wood-framed, swinging mirror mounted on a base fitted with small drawers for toilet articles; designed to sit atop a chest of drawers; very popular through late Victorian times.

Sheffield Plate Invented in the middle of the eighteenth century as a desirable substitute for solid silver; the technique

SHAVING MIRROR

involves sandwiching a layer of copper between thin layers of sterling silver; it is still being made, using modern machine equipment for quantity production and economy; plated silver shows wear but it can be replated when necessary.

Sheraton, Thomas (England, 1751–1806) Not only an expert stylist and designer of his times, but also a teacher of architecture and drawing; he was one of the first major cabinetmakers to design dual-purpose furniture; other notable contributions are the Pembroke table, the secretary/desk with upper bookcase section, satinwood inlays, and the pleasing mixture of mahogany and fruitwood. (*Illustration page 152.*)

Shibui Principle A recently popular-

151

SHERATON DESIGNS

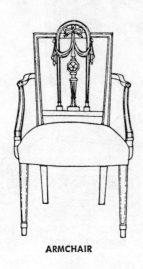

ARMCHAIR

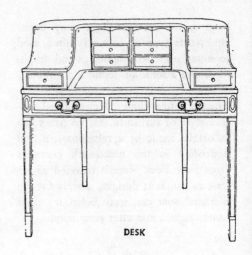

DESK

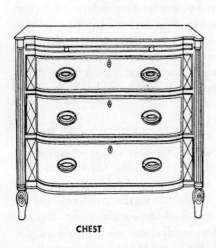

CHEST

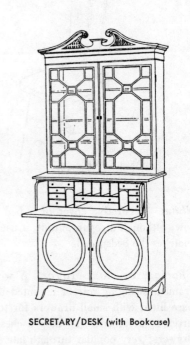

SECRETARY/DESK (with Bookcase)

ized concept for all that is subdued, refined, and tasteful according to Japanese design principles. In its purest sense, Shibui describes a decorative attitude that rejects all but low-key colors; admits few, if any, sharp contrasts of color or surface; fosters subtle, scarcely apparent surface texture; upholds the tenet that "less is more," preferring to contemplate one perfect accessory in an environment of perfect peace than be surrounded by a clutter of several simultaneously engrossing interests which may be in conflict with each other.

Shield-back Chair Hepplewhite chair design featuring open, wood back shaped like a shield; generally with upholstered seat; used mainly on dining-room and side chairs. (*See* Hepplewhite.)

Shoji Panels Individual screen panels usually made of some translucent material such as rice paper framed in black lacquer; the Japanese method of dividing a room with movable partitions; shoji panels are often used in contemporary interiors instead of curtains and drapery to screen windows effectively and attractively.

Shutters, see *Louvers*

Silent Butler An oval or oblong box-like container with a hinged lid and a projecting handle; for collecting cigarette ashes from several trays at one time; for picking up bread crumbs at the table; silver or other metals.

Silhouette Miniature portrait, usually in profile, cut out of black paper with manicuring scissors, or outlined in black and filled in with black ink; a favorite fad and hobby in the early 1800s and into Victorian times; most silhouettes are head-and-shoulders depth, although some include family groups and landscapes.

SILHOUETTE

Sisal A fiber made from the tough leaves of the agave plant that grows in most tropical climates; woven, it is used for lightweight summer rugs; generally reversible with pattern on each side.

Sleeping Alcove Present-day urban apartment adjunct—the L-shaped recess set off from the living room; with a convertible sofa, it becomes a bedroom or guest quarters; or the area is put to use as a dining room or even as a home office.

153

Sleigh Bed A French Empire design adapted and given greater popularity by Duncan Phyfe and other American cabinetmakers; its high, deeply carved headboard and footboard resemble the curved construction of a sleigh.

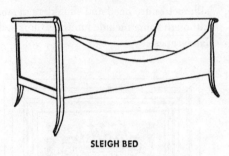

SLEIGH BED

Slipcovers Removable fabric covers for upholstered furniture; zippers, snappers, tie tapes are customary fasteners to ensure neat tailoring; fabrics are a matter of preference—sailcloth, denim, ticking, twill, linen, cretonne, chintz, etc. are all suitable; although there are ready-made covers (mostly of knitted or stretch fabrics) on the market, they cannot be expected to fit as well or to lend as much distinction of color and pattern as custom-tailored styles; keeping upholstered furniture "in the muslin" and having several sets of slipcovers in varied colors and design themes can provide pleasant changes of pace not only seasonally but throughout the year.

Slipper Chair A small-scaled boudoir chair with or without arms; usually with pleated or ruffled skirt, quilted or tufted fabric cover.

Slipware Pottery decorated with slip, or liquid clay; motifs and borders are built up, layer by layer, into a bas-relief; slip may be hand-painted in colors different from the body glaze; popular in Colonial America.

SLIPPER CHAIR

Sofa Bed Dual-purpose sofa which opens out to form a bed or a pair of twin beds; made in almost every known traditional, provincial, and contemporary style with coverings that range from elaborate cut velvet to wet-look vinyl.

Soufflé Dish A straight-sided oval or round bake-serve dish; outside is usually ribbed or fluted; china, earthenware, or heat-proof glass.

Spade Foot A late eighteenth-century simplified foot used in Sheraton and

Hepplewhite designs; it is a tapered terminal to a four-sided leg on chairs and occasional tables.

Spatterdash A spotted pattern created by shaking or gently tapping a paintbrush so that random blobs of paint drop off; used on wood floors, as a glaze on informal pottery; multicolor or monotone effects.

Spinet Gracefully styled, small upright piano; it is compact and takes little space in the average-size apartment living room.

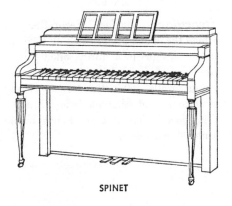

SPINET

Splat A shaped piece of wood—fiddle, vase, figure 8, lyre, etc.—that forms the center back panel of a chair.

Splayed Leg Chair leg that inclines outward at a gentle slope; prevalent during the English Regency; a characteristic Duncan Phyfe feature.

Split Bamboo Blinds Window coverings made of horizontal strips of bamboo that are cut match-stick thin to inch wide; bamboo shades roll up on tapes; usually in natural color; less formal

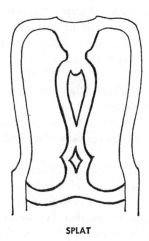

SPLAT

than venetian blinds, they have a summery look.

Spode English manufacturer of china and earthenware since 1770; the selfsame factory in the Midlands is still producing fine quality dinnerware and decorative objects.

Spool Turning An ingenious carved trim that looks like a column of wooden spools; an American Empire and Early Victorian fashion for the complete bed, headboard and footboard, the posts on a whatnot, table legs; also called Jenny Lind style in honor of the famous singer.

SPOOL TURNING

155

Spun Silk, Spun Rayon Fabric woven from short fiber lengths; it creates a slightly fuzzy surface with random thick-and-thin effects.

Stabile Present-day art-circle definition of an abstract, stationary sculpture made of sheet metal and with no moving parts; the opposite of a mobile.

Stacking Tables, Stools, Chairs Three-legged, round wood tables (double as stools) are contoured to stack one atop another so that five or six occasional tables can be stored in the space of one; chairs are usually made of molded plastic or wood, set on V-shaped metal frames.

STACKING TABLES

Staffordshire Ware Pottery and china made in the historic center of English manufacturing; there are miniature sculptures, tiny flower bouquets, groups of "personality" figurines—typical subject matter for this colorful hand-crafted ware.

Standish An elaborate inkstand composed of a footed tray with a shallow trough for pens, two inkwells, and sometimes a small drawer; made of silver, bronze, brass, papier-mâché, and other materials combined with cut glass.

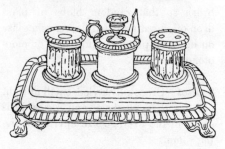

STANDISH

Stenciling Surface decoration in which the colors are brushed on through cutout designs in a sturdy, oiled paper; used on chair backs, dressers, trunks, chests, walls, cabinets, etc.; especially American and characteristic of many Hitchcock chairs and Pennsylvania Dutch furnishings.

STENCILING

156

Step Table An occasional table in the form of two or three setback steps; the top surface may be covered with tooled leather.

STEP TABLE

Sterling Silver The standard established in 1560 during the reign of Elizabeth I; it designates that 925 parts out of each 1,000 must be of pure silver; the remaining 75, of a base metal, usually copper.

Stiegel Glass A pre-Revolutionary glass from a Pennsylvania factory which was a prolific source of both utility and decorative glass objects; most of the existing examples of original eighteenth-century production are in museums or are greatly prized personal possessions; Stiegel's designs influenced his own colleagues and still are the reference material most often consulted by contemporary designers; characteristic is a deep blue color, frequently stippled with opaque white, engraved, or enameled; dark green, red, and amethyst were also used.

Stippling The method of achieving a rough-textured surface on plaster or paint; freshly applied plaster is patted with a coarse brush or a piece of crumpled burlap to give stucco, plaster, or wall paint the desired rustic effect.

Storage Units Any chest, cabinet, shelf-and-drawer furniture combination may rightly be called a storage unit; a *storage wall* is an assemblage of several such elements that can be a room-wide arrangement; it may be freestanding, pole-suspended or wall-hung from a variety of dowels, rabbets, etc.

Stretcher Horizontal strips of wood that connect chair or table legs where the extra structural support is needed.

STRETCHER

Strié A random streaky effect in woven fabric; a variation of jaspé. French word for streak. (*See* Jaspé.)

Stucco For interior and exterior use, a plaster finish made of cement, sand, and lime applied wet; used on inside walls, it has a rough texture with visible brush marks; gives a Californian or Mediterranean look.

Student Lamp The generic term for a table or desk lamp that gives glareless light, which can be focused on book or papers; some duplicate a favorite Victorian oil lamp with brass base and green glass globes; others include frosted glass spheres, draftsman's clamp-on-swing-away types, tôle-shaded *bouillotte* styles, and a host of avant-garde designs for contemporary room schemes.

STUDENT LAMP

Studio Couch A 30-inch upholstered mattress and box spring used as a day bed; with two or three boxy cushions or bolsters placed against the wall for comfort and back support.

Style vs. Fashion A style is the particular way of expressing a basic design. For example, a chair is a basic design and there are many styles of chairs. Fashion is the popular expression of a style and usually engenders many versions of it. For example, a chair with a bamboo-carved frame, if popular, will be made in many versions. Styles survive and fashions fade.

Suede Cloth Wool, cotton, and even paper are given a soft, lightly napped surface in imitation of suede leather by means of flocking.

Suite Furniture sold as a complete set of matching pieces for a specific room; a short-cut route to decoration, frowned on by professional interior designers as monotonous, limiting.

Sunburst The contours of a stylized sun and its rays fashioned into a wall decoration made of wood, metal, plaster, etc.; often gilded; sometimes used as the encircling frame for a round wall clock.

SUNBURST

Swag, see Festoon

Swatch A decorator's term for a small sample cutting of fabric, carpet, wallpaper, or paint color; often measures about 3 inches×5 inches; larger cuttings—a yard or so—are called "memo" samples and are loaned to decorators and not given gratis as swatches usually are.

Sycamore A wood of reddish color; when stained gray, the wood is known as harewood; lacy markings on a smooth close grain; hard yet lightweight; it has an unfortunate tendency to warp unless correctly seasoned; used as a solid wood for all exposed surfaces and face veneers.

T U

T

Tabouret Small round upholstered stool or bench introduced during the first quarter of the eighteenth century; French for stool.

Tabriz Rug Ivory or pale beige ground; dainty pastel allover motifs with intricate surrounding border; thinner and more delicate than other Oriental-style rugs; Tabriz rugs recede into the background and are adaptable to various styles of decoration; made in Tabriz, Iran.

T-cushion A shaped, loose cushion for an upholstered chair or sofa with projecting sections that curve around the front of the arms.

Taffeta A smooth lustrous fabric of plain weave; silk, rayon, nylon, or a blend of fibers; very adaptable for draperies, bedspreads, curtains, pillows, and any home-fashion item where a luxurious, feminine but crisp appearance is required.

Tallboy, see Highboy

T-CUSHION

Tambour A drum-shaped occasional table. A sheer muslin fabric which has been embroidered on a drum-shaped hoop, a tambour. A flexible type of closure for desks and cabinets in place of a hinged stationary one; the old-fashioned roll-top desk is an example of a type of tambour construction. The French word for drum. (*Illustration page 164.*)

163

TAMBOUR

blends, measuring spoons, etc.; tea chests were often lined with gold- or silver-printed Chinese decorative papers; of incredible sheerness these became, not surprisingly, known as tea chest designs; tea was costly even as late as the nineteenth century, so there was a real need for these special, moisture-resistant, pilfer-proof containers.

Tantalus An open-frame wood stand in which liquor bottles can be locked up; named after a disobedient ancient Greek king whom the gods punished by never allowing him to grasp anything he reached for.

Tapestry-type Rug Contemporary needlework-type accent rugs made in Spain and Portugal; peasant designs, stylized abstract motifs; a complete color palette includes primaries and pastels; many of these rugs are lined with heavy linen. (*See* Alpujarra and Arraiolo rugs.)

Tea Caddy, Tea Chest, Teapoy With the growing acceptance of tea as a social beverage toward the end of the seventeenth century, a number of useful accessories came into household use; the *tea caddy*, a silver or porcelain canister was perhaps the least pretentious; the *tea chest*, a larger, more important boxlike chest with small drawers and a lock to protect the precious contents; and the *teapoy*, a three-legged wood stand topped with a hinged chest that was compartmented to hold various

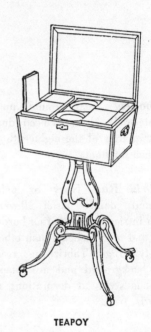

TEAPOY

Tea Cart A tiered table on wheels; wood, metal, plastic, glass, and combinations of these; today, the cart does more than serve tea, it is a practical adjunct to the maidless household—carrying china, glassware, casseroles, beverages, etc. from kitchen to table; an attractive and decorative piece of furniture; many traditional styles have drop leaves that create a full-size tea table around which chairs can be placed.

164

Teak A wood of golden to dark-brown color; hard, heavy, medium-grained with a slight pattern; highly resistant to swelling, shrinking, warping, attacks by termites; used a great deal for contemporary furniture designs, wall paneling; particularly well suited to marine use because of its unusual qualities.

Tear Glass An air bubble is blown into the base or stem of a drinking glass or vase to form a singular type of decoration.

Template A decorating aid which allows plan or room arrangement to be made to actual scale; the equipment is graph paper and a collection of tiny, silhouetted furniture items; graph is usually ½ inch- or ¼ inch-to-the-foot scale with cutouts scaled accordingly; windows, doors, wall jogs can be accurately measured and marked on the graph; cutout furniture items can be placed in position; the foolproof method of buying furnishings to a plan of what a given room will accommodate.

Terra Cotta The familiar, hard, red-orange clay used for informal pottery, flower pots, small primitive sculptures, building bricks; unless decorated in bright peasant-art style, it is usually kept unglazed; Italian for cooked earth.

Terrazzo Highly polished bits of marble or stone, or specially molded ceramic tiles make this colorful hard-surface flooring; used indoors in Mediterranean climates because it remains cool;

it is also practical for outdoor use; random patterns are duplicated in vinyl floor coverings by several companies.

Terrestrial Globe A full-color revolving representation of the earth; set into a wooden stand of table height, or in miniature scale for use on a desk; it is a Renaissance innovation that became a favored accessory for the eighteenth-century study or library; today's versions rotate, revolve, light up.

TERRESTRIAL·GLOBE

Tester Bed, see Four-poster Bed

Tête-à-tête A sofa the size of a love seat whose seat sections face each other; a typical Victorian pleasantry, it has a heavily carved frame surrounding a luxurious covering—brocade, damask, velvet. Literally, the French for head to head.

165

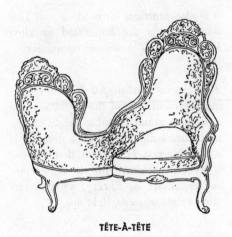

TÊTE-À-TÊTE

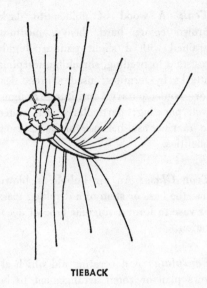

TIEBACK

Ticking Firmly woven cotton heavy enough for mattress covers; its traditional narrow pencil stripes make it equally adaptable for slipcovers, wall covering, and other decorative uses.

Tieback A loop of matching fabric, a rigid metal arm, or a cord that holds draperies and curtains open and drawn to each side of a window.

Tiffany Glass Decorative glassware designed by Louis Comfort Tiffany (a member of the family of jewelers) between 1890 and 1910; prized today as an important collector's item because of its rarity; the vases, pitchers, goblets, and other objects in their exotic iridescent colorings are marked either with the word "favrile" (handmade) or with the initials "LCT"—none other is authentic.

Toby Jug China or pottery mug in the form of a plump, jolly-faced, seated man wearing an eighteenth-century tricorn hat; he holds a beer mug and clay pipe; storybook characters like the Mad

Hatter of *Alice in Wonderland* and other personalities are satirized as Tobies; all are hollow and may be used as pencil holders, cream pitchers, small vases, etc.

TOBY JUG

Toile de Jouy A cotton muslin or percale plain-woven fabric printed with rural vignettes, scenes of eighteenth-century life; one color is used on an off-white or natural-color ground; named

166

after the town of Jouy in France where it was first produced.

Tôle Metal, usually tin, painted over in one opaque color and then decorated in another; lamp bases, trays, wastepaper baskets, hampers, etc.

Tone on Tone A darker shade of the ground color used to delineate a pattern on carpet, fabric, or wallpaper.

Tooled Leather Florentine-originated decorations on leather; the design is tooled with a special implement, then the routed-out tracery or border is filled in with metallic gold; for table and desk tops.

Topiary Art Bushes, trees, shrubs clipped into fantastic shapes (animals, mythological creatures, abstractions) by the skilled hands of imaginative gardeners; in large, formally landscaped "show-places"; present-day plastic foliage is also trimmed in these amusing forms and set into decorative planters for use in foyers, etc.

Torchère A standing lamp in the form of a large candleholder or lantern; up to five feet tall; electrified or made for candlelight.

Torte Plate Decorated glass plate that is set on a stemmed base; for serving and displaying cakes and sandwiches; *torte* is German for cake.

TORTE PLATE

TOPIARY

Traditional Style In decoration, whatever is not of its own time; period vs. modern styles; traditional schemes cling to faithful reproduction of Early American, French Court or Provincial styles, English chintzes, Chippendale, etc. in an effort to re-create an atmosphere of elegance.

Trapunto A type of quilting used on furniture covers, bedspreads, closet accessories, pillows; rows of machine stitching outline the pattern; then cord or padding is inserted between the rows to produce a raised dimensional effect.

Traverse Rod A metal curtain and drapery fixture which allows fabric to be drawn across the entire window by means of a set of cords and pulleys.

Travertine A limestone rock used as a facing material since Roman times; light cream color with an uneven surface texture; used for table tops.

Trefoil Motif shaped like a three-leaf clover; *quatrefoil* is a four-leaf version; both are commonly used ornaments on Gothic-style buildings and furnishings.

Trellis, Treillage A series of complex latticework panels, used not only in their original outdoor capacity as background for trailing vines or framework for espaliered trees, but indoors as well; they frequently double as window shutters and room dividers; the trellis pattern of openwork or pierced wood is itself the inspiration for many wallpaper and fabric prints; *treillage,* the French word for trellis, is the form more often used in decorating language.

Trestle Table Prevailing table structure of the Middle Ages, a removable board top was placed on a pair of folding supports (trestles); not until the sixteenth century was the planked top permanently fixed to a base of trestles and stretchers.

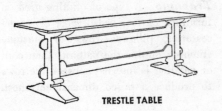

TRESTLE TABLE

Triptych Originally, an altar painting or an icon made of three hinged panels, the two side pieces folding over the center panel; today, the term also refers to a three-way make-up mirror on a dressing table.

TRIPTYCH

Trivet Three-legged stand protects the table surface from heat and moisture; using a variety of materials—solid silver, pine, brass; many have pierced and chased patterns.

Trompe l'Oeil The French phrase means fools the eye; wherever an effect of marble, fine wood, mineral, etc. was desired and the high cost or scarcity

168

of the genuine material prevented its lavish use, simulated effects were achieved through skillful painting; for witty decoration, realistic illustrations of clothing and accessories are painted on the front of a chest of drawers to fool the eye into believing that real properties are untidily tumbling out.

Trumeau   A tall, narrow-framed mirror with a landscape or group portrait painted across its top section; originally, scaled to be placed between a pair of windows or above a fireplace; today, the trumeau is hung wherever a decorative accessory is wanted; sometimes designers replace the original painting with enamel abstractions or with colorful ceramic plaques.

TRUMEAU

Trundle Bed   A carry-over from Colonial times, currently brought up-to-

date as a convenience item; practical for families living in limited quarters —a single bed of slightly smaller dimensions slides under another when not in use, like a large drawer.

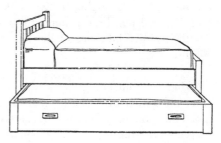

TRUNDLE BED

Tub Chair   Although it is of eighteenth-century origin, the tub chair is a familiar contemporary shape; it has wider-than-high dimensions; arms and back of the same height; plumply upholstered, pillowed, or made with tight-seat construction.

Tubular Metal Construction   Even though tubular furniture is considered a twentieth-century innovation, it has actually been in use since the 1830s; Bauhaus-trained designer Marcel Breuer is credited with developing the present technique of shaping extruded steel or aluminum tubing into continuous framework.

Tudor Period (England, 1500–58) It was the swashbuckling era of Henry VIII in England and Francis I in France, and the first time furniture was made with some semblance of beauty, comfort, engineering, as well as for sheer utility; rich upholstery fabrics

169

make an initial appearance, as do functional cupboards and storage chests, peg and dowel construction, the discovery of oak and walnut as woods with graining that was ornamental in itself; although the entire period focuses attention on an emerging native style, both England and France were still under the massive influence of the Italian Renaissance.

Tufting A modern process derived from the action of a sewing machine; more than 80 per cent of present-day carpets are tufted; yarn is pulled through backing much like candlewick embroidery; yarns are inserted by thousands of electronically controlled needles; tufts are sealed to back with latex rubber coating; every type of design including embossed effect is possible.

Tulipwood An alternate name for magnolia.

Tupelo Wood that is white-gray to gray-beige in color; ribbonlike markings when quartered; tends to excessive warping, therefore is used mainly in small areas, for concealed parts, framework.

Tureen A deep, covered dish with side handles, used for serving soups and stews; colorful and ornamental, often molded in the shape of birds, fruit, vegetables; also made of silver or stainless steel; can have an opening in the lid to allow for insertion of a curved ladle; with their customary matching trays, tureens often are used as the centerpiece of a table setting.

TUREEN

Turning The craftsman's term for shaping furniture parts on a lathe; for legs, posts, twisted and spiral railings, etc.

Tuxedo Sofa A tailored sofa style; the back is sometimes given a slight backward pitch; arms and back are of the same height; fully upholstered or framed in wood.

Twill Tight diagonal weave; solid colors mainly in neutral shades, but brilliant tones are also available.

U

Umbrella Table A beach or lawn table of rustic wood or metal with a center opening to hold a large, colorful canvas umbrella.

Undercoat A very thin preliminary coat of the final wall paint or stain to be applied.

Underglaze Decoration Patterns that are applied to china and earthenware before the final glazing and firing; this ensures permanence of design over long periods of time, dishwasher cleansing.

Urn A two-handled vase with a domed lid; most urns follow classical Greek and Roman forms; many are made of fine hand-painted porcelain with medallion decoration.

URN

V W Y Z

V

Valance An overdrapery treatment made of shaped wood or of draped, pleated, or shirred fabric; the valance hides fixtures and hardware and adds a finishing touch to the window.

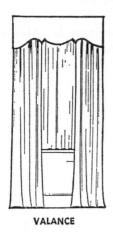

VALANCE

Vanity Table, see Poudreuse

Vat Dyes Vat-dyed decorative fabrics are boilable and sun-fast; any solid-color or patterned weaves chosen for slipcovers, draperies, table toppings should bear this information or guarantee imprinted on the selvage.

Velvet Its closely clipped, soft, dense pile has made velvet almost synonymous with regal luxury; many types and qualities exist today: silk, nylon, rayon, cotton (velveteen), and blends; cut velvet has a raised pattern of the pile—monotone or multicolor—on a finely twilled ground; pressed velvet has a light-and-shade effect produced by pressing the fabric between rollers.

Veneer Thin layers of wood applied to furniture surfaces; often these are beautifully grained and have matching patterns unequaled and unattainable in solid-wood construction.

Venetian Blind Marco Polo brought previously unknown conveniences back to Italy from exploratory voyages to the Far East; among these innovations, the slatted, tape-controlled, pull-up window blind is probably the most universal means of shading a window and adjusting light; today's versions come with both vertical and horizontal slats, take advantage of numerous carefree materials—nylon, plastic, aluminum, as well as the traditional adaptable wood.

Venetian Glass Hand-blown decorative glass that may be iridescent, smoked, or with a flurry of metallic gold flecks held in suspension; pieces are sculptural, quite heavy; also called Murano glass, the name of the island just outside Venice where the factories are actually located.

Venetian Mirror No outside frame of wood or metal surrounds a Venetian mirror; instead, an ornate border of matching mirror is an integral part; usually overscale, with undulating curves, it can be the dominant attention-getter on a wall.

Vermeil A wash of gold is applied to a silver base to give the effect of solid gold without its weight or prohibitively high cost; for table flatware and art objects.

Verre Églomisé A method of decorating the underside of glass objects with metallic gold or silver paint; invented in the mid-eighteenth century by Jean-Baptiste Glomy, a Paris art dealer and picture framer; églomisé picture mats instead of paperboard were a distinctive treatment; the decoration was also used on clock faces; a simulated effect is achieved today by means of silk-screened decoration on the inside of glass trays and table glassware. The

French word *verre* means glass; *églomisé* refers to Glomy's process.

Victorian Period (England, 1837– 1900) During Queen Victoria's sixty-three-year reign, the all-encompassing style which we call Victorian was affected by changing and modifying fashion cycles much as in our own time. These changing influences inspired certain fashion obsolescence, then as now; there were the Oriental, Rococo, cottage, or rustic, look, the revived pointed-arch Gothic, and the discovery of status-building antiques; everything seemed to assume larger-than-life proportions as though new affluence could be measured according to size and weight of surrounding objects; all kinds of gadgetry, experimental items made their debut on the home-fashion scene such as adjustable chairs, folding beds, beds that disappeared into closets and cupboards, music boxes, papier-mâché accessories; woods were heavy and dense, made more so by extravagant carving; seating units were deeply tufted or primly covered with the more austere horsehair cloth; everything to which fabric could be attached bore this weight of drapery and overdrapery, bobble fringe, and braid; few, if any, surfaces were left unadorned; there was little lighthearted décor in these stern but productive, prudish but peaceful, times.

Vinyl A broad, encompassing group of plastics derived from the chemical radical ethylene; generally opaque (floor tiles, for example), or transparent (by-

VICTORIAN PERIOD

SIDEBOARD

HALL CHAIR

SOFA

ARMCHAIR

the-yard film), wet look for upholstery; vinyl may be combined with cotton yarn for better hand and appearance; all types may be printed.

Vitrine Glass fronted, but usually all glass; a shelved cabinet for displaying and housing small curios and collec-

VITRINE

tors' items; the vitrine is delicately scaled and set on slender legs.

Voile Soft sheer cotton or synthetic fiber; printed with small, dainty, sometimes documentary patterns or dyed solid colors.

Voluté Spiral-shaped, scroll-like architectural ornament profusely applied to stone work and furniture during the Baroque period.

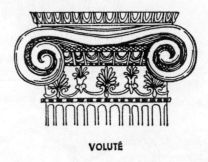

VOLUTÉ

178

W

Wainscot Wood paneling used on interior walls from baseboard up to a desired height; paint or wallpaper applied above.

Wall Bracket A quite small shelf, intricately carved, attached to a wall for displaying a clock or a piece of decorative bric-a-brac.

WALL BRACKET

Wall-bracket Table A supported drop-leaf attached to a wall; convenient wherever floor space is limited and extra surface is needed.

Wall-hung Units Cabinets, bookshelves, spice racks, etc. that are suspended from narrow wood strips nailed to a wall.

Walnut A wood of cream-yellow to dark brownish tones; figured crotch; burls; swirl and mottle markings; visible pores on a regular smooth grain; lightweight, stable, and suited to all furniture uses; makes rich veneers; versatile and adaptable.

Warp The vertical threads of a woven fabric that parallel the selvage; cross threads are called woof or weft threads.

Wash-hand Stand, or Washstand Ever since their inception in the eighteenth century, every bed/dressing room

179

featured one of these functional cabinets (sometimes they were concealed behind a folding screen); designed to hold washbasin and water pitcher (stoneware or heavy china with painted decorations), waste pail, towel bar; later versions, before built-in bath facilities became commonplace, were elaborate marble-topped Victoriana and as such are zealously collected today for use as occasional tables, planters, bars.

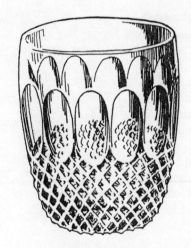

WATERFORD GLASS

WASH-HAND STAND

in upholstered furniture; the bands are crisscrossed and interwoven to absorb stress; webbing is also used to fashion backs and seats on garden furniture, beach and deck chairs.

Waterford Glass Deeply cut decorative and utility glassware made in Waterford, Ireland; decanters, vases, table accessories are specialties; most styles and cuttings are copies of eighteenth-century originals that have been manufactured continuously throughout the intervening years.

Webbing Tough cotton, plastic, or burlap bands that support the springs

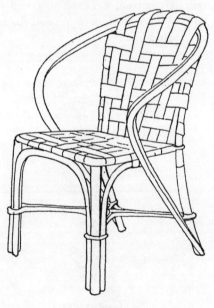

WEBBING

180

Wedgwood One of the most famous names in the realm of ceramic design; the factory established in the eighteenth century by Josiah Wedgwood is still under the management of his descendants; volumes have been written on the subject of the family and its creativity— the decorative china, the sturdy all-purpose earthenware, commemorative sculptures and urns; many innovations of style and manufacturing techniques have been attributed to Wedgwood expertise and experimentation.

WELSH DRESSER

Well-and-tree Platter Treelike branches are carved into silver, silver plate, and stainless steel serving platters so that meat juices can gather in a well at one end; oval or rectangular shapes; generally edged with a gadroon border.

WELL-AND-TREE PLATTER

Welsh Dresser Large-scale dining-room or kitchen cupboard; open, wood-backed shelves are set above a cabinet base to display china and glass.

Welting Cotton cord covered with bias fabric strips; used as a custom-tailored finish to upholstery and slip-cover seams; made to match the dominant fabric or to contrast in color.

Wet-look Materials The trend to shiny surfaces emphasized by the patent-leather look of prevalent plastic materials; all surfaces which reflect light such as glass, metal, metallic yarns, etc. contribute to the wet look.

Whipcord Like twill, a diagonal weave but heavier and coarser; rugged and long wearing; mainly neutral, solid colors.

Wickerware Furniture woven from flexible willow or reed branches; weather resistant and suited to outdoor use; may be painted or left natural color.

William and Mary (England, 1690–1702) In England during the reign of William and Mary appeared specialized furniture and furnishings for individual rooms and purposes on the decorative scene; burgeoning trade with the Far East launched a rewarding acquaintanceship with its treasures, its culture, and its civilized understanding of the importance of a surrounding environment; in the Western world, tastes began to develop and, significant for the generations to come, a new-found appreciation of comfort, design; the planned interior revealed a growing sophistication; the age of the interior designer, the craftsman, and innovator had been initiated for the future.

WILLIAM AND MARY PERIOD

SIDE CHAIR

GATE-LEG TABLE

HIGHBOY

BENCH SETTEE

SECRETARY

Williamsburg Restoration A complete city of Colonial Virginia restored to the original splendor it had as the seat of government from 1699–1779; historic sites include the governor's palace, Raleigh Tavern, church, courthouse, crafts shops, forge, etc.; a select group of American manufacturers is licensed to produce accurate reproductions of the furniture, furnishings, and accessories that are such fine examples of eighteenth-century craftsmanship; each copy bears an identifying mark, engraved or imprinted, that establishes its authenticity of detail.

WILLIAMSBURG RESTORATION (CYPHER)

Willow A wood of cream-yellow color, long flexible branches; lightweight but very durable when woven; for all indoor/outdoor casual furniture; can be painted or not.

Wilton Carpet woven on a Jacquard loom; name denotes weave, not pattern or quality; embossed and sculptured designs, using fewer than six colors; generally has a thicker pile than Axminster.

Windsor Chair A generic term for a series of chair designs that incorporate a saddle-shaped wooden seat, spindled back, splayed legs, curved and lathe-turned, supported by a stretcher; chairs were armless pull-up type or made with wide, flaring arms to hold plate, book, candle.

WINDSOR CHAIR

Wine Labels Pendants made of silver, engraved or with colored enamel designs; hung from short chains around the decanter neck; the name of the liquor is boldly lettered to identify the contents. (*Illustrations page 184.*)

Wing Chair A large, upholstered arm chair with a high back that has projecting wings at the top sides; these were added as a device to protect the sitter from drafts; popular since the seventeenth century; used traditionally in pairs at either side of a fireplace.

Wire Work Thin silver or plated wire is worked into baskets, fruit bowls, and serving dishes lined with glass; usually circular because the wire was easily bent into convex forms; popular at the close of the eighteenth century, during the English Regency, and into the present.

Writing Table A rectangular flat-topped table with a series of drawers set into the front apron; eighteenth-century French and English Regency styles.

Wrought Iron Comparatively pure form of iron (low carbon content) that is shaped by heat and hammering; less brittle than cast metal; furniture made of wrought iron is durable, weather resistant.

WRITING TABLE

WROUGHT IRON

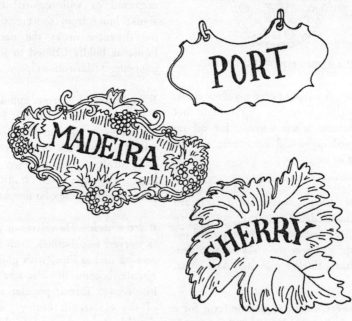

WINE LABELS

Y

Z

Yarn-dyed Yarn is dyed before being woven into fabric; opposed to piece dyeing where the finished cloth is dyed in huge vats.

Yew Fine-grained, soft-wood evergreen; of pale color with attractive red berries that are poisonous; used for inlays and decorative trim; the specific wood needed for archery bows.

Zebrawood A wood with black stripes on yellowish ground; fine smooth texture; for inlays, trimming, and veneers on all types of contemporary furniture.

Zigzag Sharp V-shaped allover motif, woven or printed; also, a braid trimming, called rickrack.

BIBLIOGRAPHY

Bedford, John, *Old Spode China*. New York, Walker & Company, 1969.
———, *Pewter*. New York, Walker & Company, 1968.
Bjerkoe, Ethel Hall, *The Cabinetmakers of America*. Garden City, N.Y., Doubleday & Company, Inc., 1957.
Comstock, Helen, *100 Most Beautiful Rooms in America*. New York, Viking Press, 1965.
Cox, Warren E., *The Book of Pottery and Porcelain*. New York, Crown Publishers, 1944.
Dauterman, Carl Christian, *Sèvres*. New York, Walker & Company, 1969.
Dennis, Jessie McNab, *English Silver*. New York, Walker & Company, 1970.
Draper, Dorothy, *365 Shortcuts to Home Decorating*. New York, Dodd, Mead, 1968.
Elville, E., *Dictionary of Glass*. London, Country Life, 1961.
Fastnedge, Ralph, *English Furniture Styles*. New York, A. S. Barnes, 1964.
Gloag, John, *A Short Dictionary of Furniture*. New York, Bonanza Books, 1965.
Grant, Ian, *Great Interiors*. New York, Dutton, 1967.
Haggar, Reginald G., *The Concise Encyclopedia of Continental Pottery and Porcelain*. New York, Frederick A. Praeger, Inc., 1960.
Haynes, E. Barrington, *Glass Through the Ages*. Baltimore, Pelican Division of Penguin Books, 1948.
Hayward, Helena, *World Furniture*. New York, McGraw-Hill Book Company, 1965.
Hicks, David, *David Hicks on Decoration*. New York, Macmillan, 1968.
Kornfeld, Albert, *Doubleday Book of Interior Decorating*. Garden City, N.Y., Doubleday & Company, Inc., 1965.
Magnani, Franco, *Modern Interiors*. New York, Universe Books, 1969.
Mankowitz, Wolf and Haggar, Reginald G., *The Concise Encyclopedia of English Pottery and Porcelain*. New York, Hawthorn Books, 1960.
O'Brien, George, *The New York Times Book of Interior Design*. New York, Farrar, Straus & Giroux, 1965.

Pevsner, Nikolaus, *Pioneers of Modern Design from William Morris to Walter Gropius.* New York, Museum of Modern Art, 1949.

Savage, George, *Porcelain Through the Ages.* New York, Pelican Division of Penguin, 1963

———, *Concise History of Interior Decoration.* New York, Grosset & Dunlap, 1966.

Taylor, Gerald, *Silver.* rev. ed., Baltimore, Penguin, 1964.

Tiffany Table Settings. New York, Crowell, 1960.

Varney, Carleton, *The Family Decorates a Home.* Indianapolis, Bobbs-Merrill, 1969.

Viaux, Jacqueline, *French Furniture.* New York, Putman's Sons, 1964.

NOTE: In the series called "Collectors' Pieces," Walker & Company has companion volumes to the above listed on the following subjects: *Wedgwood, Bristol, Staffordshire, Delftware, Old Worcester China, Chelsea and Derby China, Old Sheffield Plate.* These are all written by John Bedford.